CEO SYSTEM

The Hidden Culture

VAIDHAL

No part of this book may be reproduced or redistributed in any form or by any electronic or mechanical means, including information storage and retrieval systems, without permission in writing from the author or the publishers.

Ibukku is an auto-publishing company. The content of this work is the responsibility of the author and do not necessarily reflect the views of the publisher.

CEO System
Published by Ibukku.
www.Ibukku.com
Graphic design: Índigo Estudio Gráfico
Copyright © 2018 VAIDHAL
ISBN Paperback: 978-1-64086-243-2
ISBN eBook: 978-1-64086-244-9
Library of Congress Control Number: 2018957779

THE MAGICAL STADIUM IN ZAPOPAN, JALISCO. It was Jackie's fifth job interview in that place. "So many interviews," she thought. She continued completing her access at the A7 gate at one of the stadium entrances. "If someone had told me a few months ago that I could be working here, I would have laughed out loud. I don't really like soccer", she continued thinking without looking up and feeling how that big gray elephant encircled her. "The stadium is so huge, I hope they decide soon to tell me if they hired me or not. Just imagine that I could be the Operation Director in this place full of joy", That was her last thought before focusing on her next interview.

Jackie with a lot of effort had just finished her masters in one of the most prestigious universities in the country, and she was looking for a way to give her family a better life. The internal struggle with her husband over labor situations was a difficult thing, but nothing she could not handle.

Her husband was somewhat "old-fashioned", rooted in their family customs and traditions, with two children growing up. All this made her doubt about the possibility of accepting a job with major responsibilities, but her determination to offer her family a better future made her feel and stay firm in demonstrating to herself her capacity to be part of a great business group.

It was 11 o'clock in the morning and after almost an hour and a half of chatting with one of the group Directors, Jackie left smiling through the front door of that stadium. She was certain she'd made a good impression, and better yet, because the person who interviewed her said he could possibly be her line directive.

Jackie headed to the parking lot and went down the stairs where she found Phillipe Livier, a classmate from the same generation as her when she was studying her masters. Phillipe was French and a quite attractive man. As soon as she saw him and crossed smiles Jackie could not hide the blush on her face.

"Hello Jackie! What a pleasure to see you, and what are the odds of us catching up in here," he told Jackie showing his white and bright smile.

"Hello Felipe, yes, what a coincidence, it's nice to see you". And so, Jackie continued her way to finding her car rapidly.

"This is not possible". Jackie thought. Phillipe, that cocky little French guy was here. "Surely, he's here for filling up the same position, damn it!" Suddenly Jackie felt an unexpected and drastic change in her beautiful brunette skin. Immediately, she thought grabbing Phillipe's arm and tell him that she would be the one to take the job.

She jumped in her car, moved the rear view mirror to check her lipstick was still alright, and then she stopped to look at her own eyes, and out loud she said to herself, "Everything will be fine." She recalled that moment she'd just lived, precisely that moment at the end of the interview shaking hands with who would be her next boss, he asked her one last question, "Well, Jackie. To finish this meeting, I would like you to describe yourself but using only one word." The Director warned her.

That took her by surprise, but she responded firmly with a beautiful smile, "Evolving." Now the surprised one was he. The answer was immediate with steady steps and with self-confidence, she walked away closing the door of the office behind her

Jackie was still sitting inside her vehicle, in front of the rearview mirror, her curly brown hair swirled at the sight of her hazel eyes, and at that moment only her laughter was heard flooding the place. She was imagining the answer that Felipe could have given when they asked him to describe himself in a single word, and with a mocking laugh she said to herself, "I'm sure he would say something like: tall, fit and I use Armani suits", or in the best case maybe he would ask, "Could you repeat the question please?"

A couple of seconds later, Jackie finally left the place, her smile came back to her face, all beautiful and confident like always. Already much calmer, she arrived at the nearest mall. She had to make several purchases for her children before heading back home. She had always overseen buying food and supplies her family needed. Time there seemed to go faster somehow, that without noticing it was already lunch time and she hadn't finished shopping yet. Nevertheless, she continued enjoying the moment. She was still amazed at how she had survived the years during her master's studies. At college it was common of her classmates to ask her, "How can you do it Jackie? How can you work, study and in addition live in two different places at the same time?" She just laughed and answered that she had three different phone numbers and that each of them helped her in different situations.

Jackie was coming down the electric stairs which will lead her to the food court, when she suddenly listened her cell phone ringing, she felt her accelerated pulse and looked for the phone inside her bag before answering hastily, "Hello? ". She answered just before the phone stopped ringing.

"Good afternoon, I'm Patricia Mercado, Omni-Humano's Development Director, do you remember me Jackie? We had a talk some weeks ago," continued that woman with a pretty nice and feminine voice.

"Yes, of course Ms. Mercado, it is nice to hear you. What can I do for you?" Jackie replied rushed.

"Thank you, Jackie, before anything please call me Patty; besides We practically work together." That nice voice told her.

"Absolutely Patty," Jackie said. She felt those words would make her jump for joy and excitement! She could not speak any further, she simply stood there holding the phone.

"Listen carefully Jackie, Esteban, the engineer, you remember him? He's our manager has just given me instructions to call you and inform you what's required for you to get to the Red Dragons Sport Club at nine o'clock in the morning. So, what do you think Jackie? Welcome to Omni-Humano's Group. Congratulations, it is a great challenge and We are sure you are the one for this job," Patty continued explaining.

After a couple of seconds and with a dry mouth Jackie replied, "Great Patty! Could you confirm with Engineer Esteban that I'll be there tomorrow." Jackie was so happy for that remarkable opportunity. At times her rational mind was reluctant to accept great news.

"One more thing, Jackie," Patricia added before hanging up the phone. In this precise moment Jackie was feeling like her legs were not able to hold her own body. There was a short pause. With a little bit more of awareness Patty could've noticed her accelerated breathing. "This is an executive position in the group, so tomorrow morning the engineer will give you a sealed envelope with the information that I need you to sign as soon as possible. There, you will find: your contract, a checkbook and a business credit card application which you must complete and return with all the documents duly signed. The moment you receive the envelope, please contact me again to explain everything and to help you not having any problem nor doubt. For now, that's all Jackie, you already have my contact information, and well, welcome to the group again." Jackie ended the phone call and almost without noticing she was getting into her favorite restaurant. She was still stunned by Patricia's tone of voice.

"That woman, what a strength is in her voice, how could I say yes to everything she asked me? It was as if I had been bewitched by her words. What has happened to the chief operating officer's position? What has happened to me? Why can I just say Yes with all my strength and all my energy?" she thought.

Jackie had some free time and this news had woken up her appetite. She ordered her favorite dish. It was time to celebrate! Thus, she put all her questions aside and continue enjoying her meal.

Her smile was so big and beautiful that a man sitting at the table in front of her started flirting discretely. It wasn't common that such an attractive and elegant woman was eating alone. She didn't even respond to the man. Her thoughts were only about the fact that she was going to be the Managing Director of that huge Sports Club at that wonderful city.

"RED DRAGONS" SPORT CLUB.

The following day, at exactly 8 o'clock am., Jackie was on her way. She had not been able to sleep very well at night due to the discussion with her husband Miguel, he kept insisting that Jackie could not maintain the right order at home and at the same time her job at the Sports Club. The navigation system of her car showed the approximate duration of the trip, it indicated 55 minutes of travel.

She and her family lived near the university and around the magical stadium. But the Sports Club was right on the opposite side of the city. Although at that time there was a bit of traffic, she had to hurry. She did not want to be late for her official presentation to the team. She could tell the road she had to go through to get there was of a low social level, as well as the place where the club was located. "How can this influential club be here?" she thought.

When the navigation system indicated she was just a few miles from her destination, Jackie was surprised to see a large perimeter fence labeled by a beverage company, in some of its parts there was graffiti unusually grotesque, on the upper edge very close to logos of the team they had an electrified net that made it look very different to what she had been expecting to see.

After she arrived at the main parking lot, Jackie identified herself to the security guard, nevertheless she could not enter because of the excessive number of cars that were already in the place. The guard pointed out she could use the employees' parking lot, so she decided to drive around the place and go to the site that he had mentioned.

She had gotten in through the back door of the facilities and managed to park her car in an empty spot that she found nearly at the entrance of the parking lot, when almost at onces he heard a horn that caused her a startling shock. Jackie did not understand the gestures that the person inside the car stopped just behind her car was doing.

Then the person behind the glass of that other vehicle began to speak with a rather rude voice telling Jackie she was parked at a place that was not indicated for her. "Look darling, you're using my parking spot, if you are visiting someone or whatever you need to use the section over there, you know at the back of the place." It was a woman with short dark hair with a strong voice and eyes covered by sunglasses.

Slightly ashamed, but also mad at her for the way that woman had spoken, Jackie responded, "I did not realize that there was a sign indicating not to park, but if you don't want someone else to occupy your parking space, you should arrive earlier." Visibly annoyed, she got away from the place, ignoring the way the black-haired woman intoned the horn of her car. She continued her path, but something caught her attention. She stopped at the pool area and observed a water slide's ruins that used to be one of the central attractions of the place. She kept walking by the yards and gardens until she finally reached the front door. During her hole trail she was kind of surprised to see just one or two people around. "So, why in the world did the parking lot was so crowded?" Jackie wondered.

She had finally arrived at the Director's office. It had been complicated and bumpy to get there besides, her feelings and senses were mixed because of observing the club's state, Jackie felt sad to see the lamentable conditions of the place, but at the same time she was figuring out the best form get the Club back to life.

All its furniture was old, like that of an old house in disuse. Her heart started to beat harder and faster when suddenly the huge doors of the office opened, it was Esteban, one of the managers of the group and now her line manager. "Jackie, it's so good to see you again. Go ahead, come in, from now on this will be your new office," he indicated her with an air of presumption.

"Thanks engineer, it was a little complicated to arrive. I did not know this side of the city, and the truth is, if it wasn't for the navigation system, I would have been lost," Jackie answered.

"Yes, I know, Jackie, but now you're here, hence let me tell you a little bit about this place. It was one of the first sport centers the team acquired, here we've got a soccer school, a small hotel with about 30 rooms, several professional soccer fields, a semi-Olympic pool, six tennis courts, four squash courts, five pelota courts. So, as you can see Jackie this is a very varied and complete club. Right here, where we want you to work with us. You'll be the one in charge of the proper functioning of the place and obviously continuing with the development of it," Esteban explained patiently.

"Let me explain everything better, and I hope to be clear. The person who's in charge of the club now has a new challenge. This person has worked for the future of this place. I'll like to inform you too that there are also construction plans of how it might look when we finish the hole transformation. For instance, the tennis courts will be moved, the pool will be fixed. Therefore, I hope that, step by step and little by little with you being in charge, you finish giving this great project its shape," The manager argued.

"Wow, this is really a great project Engineer. I feel very proud of the trust and confidence you've given me to continue everything. When Patty told me about a new challenge I felt kind of confused, but now that I've listened to you, I'm certainly getting it. In fact," Jackie continued. "When I first got here I noticed that most of the site needed, in my opinion of course, one than other adjudgment so it can improve its appearance." Explained Jackie with a comfort tone in her voice.

"I'm glad you understand the situation of the club, nonetheless it's not only the appearance Jackie. It also must be one-hundred percent functional. To achieve this, remember you must join a work team. I encourage you to see it as the opportunity to create a new concept in sports clubs. Just imagine that once transformed and fully operational, this Club will set an example to stablish more clubs in different cities where the team's fans feel happy and pleased to form part of," Esteban kept explaining to Jackie.

"Of course, Engineer, I couldn't agree with you more. Soccer in this country is a sport with so many fans. I suppose making them feel part of this team would be something phenomenal," Jackie confirmed.

"That's right, Jackie, this club has a lot to offer, so I'm sure you're the right person to do it. Your experience in other companies and your own-Evolution were the things that convinced me to hire you to continue the project," Esteban finished explaining.

Jackie remained thoughtful and felt the challenge in the same way in which Esteban was posing it. A connection between them began. Esteban got up from the desk and they went to the boardroom.

In that place there were 12 chairs all around and 2 more in the headboards. The room was full of construction plans and architectural designs of all the alterations planned for the club.

They were moving from one place to another as Esteban was showing the plans to Jackie and every time He opened one he was filled with pride and joy pointing out the way in which things should be done. "Jackie, I hope you understand that this project requires a substantial investment in time and resources, therefore, it has been kept a secret from the people who work here and in the same way from the members of the club. The group's board has told me that it will remain a secret until everything is ready to start. We will put a huge facade in the main entrance to show everyone the new concept of sports club of which they will be part," Esteban explained. "From this moment on, you'll work hand by hand with your team, and I'll come weekly to verify the advances you'll have made in the scheme. I want you to create a control panel in which you can see the progress percentage of each of the plans. Now, if you will, let's take a tour around the club facilities before the meeting we'll have with all the managers in charge. There, your official presentation to the team will take place, and of course you will see more things including some particularities that you are already familiarizing yourself with," he finished, taking out a handkerchief to dry the sweat from his forehead.

"He seems a little nervous, Jackie's charm made him babble every now and then. What could He mean with particularities?" Jackie thought to herself.

Esteban approached to the windows of the meeting room and hastily closed them. The air moved all Esteban's papers and plans. Jackie smiled trying to catch everything at the same time.

After rearranging everything, they began their journey. Jackie was very cautious, just observing and listening to her new boss. Esteban was speaking in a very low voice so that nobody knew the club's big secret.

Esteban was a very courteous and kind man. They never talked about personal things. All the time they referred to the project as" The Sloughing of the Dragon scales." As it was the first time she participated in a secret project. Jackie sometimes felt a great uncertainty, but at the same time she enjoyed the passion that her boss was infecting on her.

They had breakfast at the Club's café. By the moment they'd finished their meal, they paid their bills separately and lead their way to the meeting they'll have. Every single time they walked next to any employee they said Hello to Esteban, even so Jackie realized that they did it in an odd way. She occasionally believed they ran as fast as they could after greeting him.

They arrived at the main staircase and before going up to the boardroom, Jackie told Esteban she needed to go to the restrooms for a moment. Esteban showed her the nearest one and said he would wait for her in the boardroom.

"There is something strange with the people who work here. They all seem to be justifying what they're doing," thought Jackie when she came out of the restroom. She was anxious to meet the staff with whom she would work with directly. That sensation made her not realize the state of abandonment the toilets had. Jackie took the stairs and found Alexia, her new assistant. Alexia accompanied her to the boardroom and let her in, and immediately closed the door behind her.

Already located in the right spot and in front of the boardroom table, she realized why there were so many chairs. A place this large is needed to gather fourteen people at the same time. So many people there waiting, just to meet her, it got her a slightly nervous. From the moment she entered, she quickly observed everyone present, but there was someone that immediately caught her attention.

"Go ahead Jackie come, take your seat, and let me introduce the entire team," Esteban indicated her with a firm voice. "They're the twelve managers that work in the Club. Each one of them oversees diverse areas and together they operate the place." Esteban asked every single person to introduce themselves. There was a lot of nervousness in that meeting room, and none of them seemed to want nor to draw any kind of intention to introduce themselves.

Jackie noticed the whole situation and it was she who started introducing herself. She stood up from her seat and instantly started talking in a paused form. "Good afternoon everybody. Let's fulfil this formality with a different technique. There's a lot of names and you've already known each other, the new one is me. She said to them with a firm and confident voice. So, let's start introducing the person on the right side of us, and when you do so, I'd like you to focus only on two things," Jackie explained to them trying to see everyone. "The first thing I want to know is what is the name of that person?

The next thing is, that you're only using one word to describe your co-worker. As you'll see this is a different way to get to know you. You've been working together for some time, so this whole activity should be easier for you. Jackie finished clearing up how do the presentations should be."

Meanwhile, Jackie started to walk around the table, stopped at the middle and touched one person's shoulder. Someone who strangely was familiar to her. Yes, of course, there was no doubt, that person was the same woman from the parking lot who'd made her have a very unpleasant moment. Additionally, without lowering her voice down, and trying to keep eye contact with everybody, Jackie indicated to her that she'll be the one to start. In that moment everyone remained in silence, and all the eyes were on Camila, she was the first person to start.

Camila was the accounting director, a woman with a specialization in finance. Single, well-toned body, white skin, fit, pointy-cute nose, very big and black eyes. She was always taking care of her physical appearance.

Next to her, to the right was Ricardo, the maintenance director. An architect by profession but extremely communicative. Every person there know Camila and Ricardo didn't get along, in fact, only because they were the last to arrive at the meeting that they didn't have any other option rather than to sit next to each other.

Then Camila began. She said his name was Ricardo and that she ignored how he like people to call him. Right after that, without hesitation she described Ricardo with the word "Fake." Because of that, everyone inside that office was astonished from Camila's answer, not because they agreed, but because of her audacity. Esteban was also there, and despite of the problems they all had between each other, they always tried to behave properly when an executive was there.

When she heard the description Camila made, Jackie took a few steps and asked the others to continue the presentations. She put her hands on Ricardo's shoulders, still embarrassed by the description made by his colleague, felt Jackie's hands and gave him the confidence to continue. So, when he described Martha, the human resources director, he referred to her with the word "Distracted".

What a situation, the second description of the day and again it was not pleasant at all. Jackie observed Martha's panicky expression. Martha, a middle-aged woman with long black hair, it was common for her to use a ponytail. The glasses she wore helped her disguise her ears a bit.

Esteban looked surprised at how Jackie was getting information from the managers. Although, he knew that some did not like to work together, but never imagined that they had that opinion of one another and even less that they would say it openly.

The presentations were finished and now Jackie stood in the front, quickly she said a little about herself. It was a small pause and eventually normality was returning to the table.

After finishing the presentations. everyone was changing positions in their seats, they looked a little more relaxed, the final stage had already passed. Jackie watched their faces, most of them surprised. They looked at each other without understanding what had happened.

"Before finishing our first meeting, I want to let you know that I am going to schedule individual interviews with each one of you. We are going to use the necessary time to get to know your activities in detail and as a team we will make things happen," Jackie informed the managers. Jackie thanked them for their presence and asked them to return to their activities.

Everyone in the meeting room got up almost immediately, none of them expected this greeting from the new Director. Esteban was still sitting with an expression of surprise. Jackie was standing at the door of the meeting room, saying goodbye to everyone. When she found herself facing Camila, they both looked directly into each other eyes, shook hands in an indifferent way and offered a fake smile. Jackie finished that activity and closed the door to get back to Esteban.

"And well, Engineer, what's your first impression of our first meeting?" Jackie questioned.

"Oh dear! In less than an hour you got a lot of information. I would have never imagined that the team had such opinions of themselves. I must tell you that very few times I was present at a meeting with all the directors of the club, please send me a summary of each meeting you have with them," her new boss said sharply.

"Certainly! Every Monday before midday you will receive in your e-mail, my weekly schedule, in it you will find the programming of my activities and of course all the notes from the meetings held with the team," replied Jackie with a friendly and cooperative tone.

"Excellent, Jackie, I'm really pleased with the way you're working. I must go back to the stadium. I leave you to continue creating your work plan." Esteban warmly stretched Jackie's hand and left hastily from the place.

A NEW PATH FOR THE FAMILY

The main avenue for getting back home had very heavy traffic since it was Friday night. When she traveled from one place to another, or one city to another, she was used to talk to herself out loud. That habit was a part of Jackie since her childhood, plus, listening to her thoughts made her feel accompanied.

From the moment she left her new job, she'd been driving for only ten minutes. When the traffic jam did its thing, hence it was practically a huge parking lot, she turned her head to the right and the groping on a man's wheel caught her attention. The man and Jackie exchanged looks. His eyes reminded her of Miguel's eyes. Her husband got into his angry mood during traffic and did the same wheel grouping thing.

Jackie turned on the radio. She wanted to forget that man's image that seemed to be a preview of what will come the moment she gets home.

Droplets began appearing on her windshield as the traffic began to move. She immediately breathed deeply. For some people having the rain do what it does at that precise time could've been catastrophic. However, for Jackie, she felt it as her companion. She felt in her face the previous sensation when rain is approaching. She loved that sensation, the inexplicable aroma that circles the environment. There is no other possibility, what follows is a torrential rain.

Soon Jackie already had her arm completely wet. She distracted her sight from the road for a second, under the gaze of people in other cars and feeling obligated to do so, she pressed the button so that the window glass would close leaving the rain outside. It was at that moment that she understood the way her husband talked. The rain had given her another experience more in her life.

"My conversation with Miguel must be different, there is no going back, I have to overwhelm him with all kinds of sensations, just like the rain does. I must make him feel the emotion of starting a new course in life. what we have lived has been good, but now, what follows will be much better," Jackie was still speaking loudly.

She wanted to record those words in her mind. She could feel the pleasant emotions multiplying in her thoughts. There was an emotional party inside her, she felt the strength to convince of anyone of anything standing in front of her. Concentrated on not losing that sensation, she put some music on and followed the path full of enthusiasm. After not realizing how long her journey was, she was parking in front of her house.

Her peculiar way of accompanying herself had to end, Miguel was afraid of her when she heard her talking to herself in the bathroom or when she was in the shower. That night when she got home, she hugged her family differently. That night she learned the meaning of offering an endless hug. That hug that always accompanies those who receive it. Putting aside everything she felt during the day, she just enjoyed the warmth from her home.

After tucking the children in, Jackie asked Miguel to go up to the highest part of their house. From that place you could see the stars. She took her jacket from the bag, a picture with a religious figure, put them in Miguel's hands and began reading the prayer on the back of it aloud. Jackie had worked hard to get that new job and needed her husband to help her in this new direction.

Miguel did not believe in any religion, but at that moment he could feel how Jackie's voice was leading him to a state of tranquility, that energy that he could not describe, but he liked to enjoy when she transmitted it to him.

At the end of the prayer, Jackie looked up and began to list all the things that would be best for her family, in Jackie's eyes was the reflection of the moon. She asked for those happy moments, next to her family, for those things to last longer.

That self-respect Jackie had and wanted to transmit it to her husband in those moments. She had accepted many things that bothered her about her own self, but nevertheless, she had to be tolerant with all things that she still could not evolve in it.

She explained to Miguel how many times she had to sleep alone and sad in unfamiliar places. Described some situations that she had to face alone without his support. Jackie had learned that respect and tolerance gave her the possibility to improve communication with anyone.

Miguel argued, answering that many of those times had been because she'd wanted them so. "In this family the woman must be at home taking care of her children and husband. The greatest responsibility of every married woman is to take care of her family," Miguel repeated whenever he could.

Jackie observed with sadness as her efforts were not working, she just wanted to show she could attend both responsibilities at the same time. She had done it before, now she needed to take the second step, she needed her husband's help to continue.

There is a great difference between giving support and providing help, for a long time Miguel had only supported his wife. "To support" is just to give sustenance to the other and leaving them to do something with their own means. "To help" is to cooperate in a direct and specific way so that whoever is looking to fulfill a dream can achieve it.

Jackie remembered what she had lived hours before in the middle of the traffic when the rain wet her arm. She continued insisting on overflowing Miguel completely, her efforts focused on him realizing that having a wife does not mean having a woman who needs to be there exclusively to provide help to the family and him. Being spouses should not be just the union of two rings and an invisible chain. The spouses must be partners, they can extend the chain that unites them and help each other so that they can reach whatever they decide.

    Jackie was still talking to her husband without having fully achieved what she was looking for. She had managed in previous occasions to get Miguel's support, but she knew that in this situation she had to count on his help.

MONDAY, FIRST DAY OF WORK

Jackie was jubilant for her first day of work. She switched on her thoughts and left her house early. As she was used to, she would take advantage of the time from the trip home to her new office lasted to think about that secret project Esteban had offered her.

Without a doubt it was a great challenge, however in all the plans that he'd shown her, there was none that referred to the people who worked there. For Jackie it was obvious the first difficult situation to solve, they had left out from the club's remodeling the most important thing: .People's labor quality.

The way her team of directors reacted to her presentation at the club, had left her quite uncomfortable. Her first thoughts led her to compare them with elementary school children. She remembered her school friends and began to imagine her new companions dressed in those little school uniforms. "It would have been very fun to see everyone well-groomed and well seated waiting for their new teacher," thought Jackie. She knew she had to know each one of them better, give them the necessary and know what their responsibilities were, and it would help her to be able to put together a strategy that would take her to accomplish all that the board Directors and she wanted.

Once again it was very crowded, but this time it was different, approaching the entrance. The access lane got up and immediately indicated her to go through a different lane. This access led to two places outside the main entrance of the club to preferential parking places. She drew a smile on her face, remembering the argument with Camila and no matter how hard she tried, she couldn't get that woman out of her mind

With a wide smile on her face Jackie was entering a new parking area, there was no need to take more than two steps to enter the club. In that area there was also access for disabled people, and surprisingly in that place there was a sign that said, "Only small cars."

Though, there was a security staff from the club indicating to Jackie the place where she should park. Through her truck's window she asked the staff the reason for that sign.

"Here, ma'am! Welcome, you can park your vehicle in these two places," Mr. Melquiades indicated, one of the oldest guards in the club.

"Good morning! Excuse me, but the sign says that only small cars can park," Jackie argued.

"Yes ma'am, the floor tile is new and as you can see your truck occupies more than one place, but don't worry because all the directors have parked their cars here. There's no problem," the guard said.

Without saying anything else, Jackie finished parking, got out of the car, opened the rear compartment and took a screwdriver. She began removing the "only small cars" sign by herself.

Mr. Melquiades was concerned as he didn't believe what he was seeing, but then, he shared a smile with Jackie that made them accomplices about the sign's situation.

Jackie's executive profile was based on face-to-face leadership. She did not agree with those Directors or leaders who were always behind the desk. That was boring for her and she knew that most of the times that those type of Directors had an incomplete vision of what really happened in the operative levels, right where the connection with the client is gained or lost.

As she walked to her office Jackie asked her assistant the phone extensions of all the managers. She took a deep breath and decided to initiate the calls, so she could interview each of them and write down the appointments on her schedule.

Alexia gave her the phone extensions list, almost immediately. Jackie was just getting comfortable in her chair when her phone rang letting her know Francisco Carmona, the security director, was out there and wanted to stop by to see her.

Francisco was a 55-year-old man, angry faced, with an extensive experience within the group. He was one of those people who found it hard to change their way of thinking. Francisco had been at the forefront of the first team's presence in the stadium for more than ten years, but for an unknown reason to her, for the last five years they decided to put him in charge of the club's safety instead.

Jackie stood up from her chair and headed for the door to receive her first visit. During the initial presentation meeting she saw Francisco and remembered him. He was always distant from the group, and when they described him they referred to him as "mysterious."

Francisco got in the office and immediately walked towards Jackie's desk. In his hands was a bright red folder. Jackie took a notebook and by doing a delicate move with her hand invited him to take a seat. "Good Morning Francisco, how can I help you today?"

"Good morning, Director, not much, I'm just passing by to give you the weekend's report," he answered her. Francisco gave her several files.

Jackie looked at him, "Thank you, Francisco. But before I check your report, I'd like to ask you: How are you feeling?" Jackie said directly.

Francisco opened his eyes widely, he didn't understand that type of question. A little uncertain he decided to answer, "Well, fine, thank you. There's been some minor issues with the pool from Saturday and of course Sunday. People with an expired entry-pass wanted to get in. Today half of my staff was delayed, but that's ok, I mean, same as always," explained Francisco.

"Francisco, listen carefully, okay? How are you feeling? I didn't ask how you were. Nor did I ask what those files are about," Jackie said pointing at the files on the table. Jackie got up, reached for two bottles of water from her office's mini fridge, opened hers and offered him the other one. In that moment the first interview was starting. Jackie began talking to Francisco.

She told him that she wanted to share a story that had happened to her when she was in college studying her masters. Subsequently, without losing any time she began telling her anecdote. The first day of classes was a special and interesting day for Jackie in every manner.

She began her story with a nostalgic voice, "The night before I couldn't sleep, I had just arrived at the city from a business trip and hadn't had time to look for accommodation. I was so excited to start my studies that I did not care to arrive at a guest house, but that night the owner of the place had no rooms available but allowed me to stay on the living room's floor. She handed me a mattress and some blankets. I spent the whole night without being able to close my eyes to sleep.

"Next morning already in the university, all the new students were taken to the main auditorium. There all the academic representatives were gathered dressed in their cap and gown, all of them sitting at the lower part of the auditorium, a very formal ceremony. the university's rector was in the middle. From the speakers of the place they were telling us that we should take a seat. All my classmates and I quickly settled down to start the ceremony.

"The rector raised up and said his welcoming speech. At the end of the ceremony he named each one of us and next we introduced ourselves to the whole generation. Each one of the fifty classmates went down the stairs to make their personal presentation. Each of us was given a personalized identification that should be placed on the side of the auditorium chair, and at the time of our presentation we were all asked the same question: 'Welcome. How are you? Tell us a little about yourself.'

"At that moment, being in front of that group of people, I was paralyzed by fear, and the only thing that came out of my mouth was the truth, 'I'm exhausted, and tired because I couldn't sleep last night.' The silence inside the auditorium was instant, like I'd said something wrong, everyone paid attention to my words.

"The rector once again stood up from his chair and asked me another question: 'And, how do you feel Jackie?'

"'I feel happy!' I told him. 'I'm dying to start already.' The rector's smile and words comforted me.

"'You've already started Jackie. Welcome to your new home. We will take care of your physical heath and that in your insides you keep feeling happy.' The ceremony continued, but now in a different form. Everyone answered these two questions and spoke with more self-confidence. We quickly learned the difference between how you are and how you feel. Now do you understand Francisco?" Jackie remembered that feeling and became excited like on her first day of school. She finished her story and looked for Francisco's eyes.

"Yes, I understand Director. Sometimes we say things just because, but the truth is that we don't really care what the other person answers," responded Francisco, moving his shoulders with an air of resignation.

"So, Francisco, we should put aside the false cordiality and if we really want to talk to someone, we should use those two questions. Don't you think?" Jackie said reclining her chair.

"Well, yes Director, I'm always hurried, and feeling pressured."

"Hurried? You're hurried Francisco? Let's talk about the reason why you're like that." Jackie was curious in knowing the cause.

"It's just that, the files that I came to deliver are the reports of everything that happened in the club throughout the weekend, the hours of arrival of the other Directors, and I still need to go to the soccer school to talk to Professor Erik. Next week the summer course begins, and we'll receive more than five hundred children, so I feel pressured. My co-workers do their thing just for doing them, they say they will support me, but it's always me who ends up doing all the work." Francisco talked to Jackie about all the things that made him feel pressured. most of them had to do with the reluctance of their peers towards their work in the club, but there was one comment, which caused Jackie special curiosity. "I am one of the directors who has been here longer, that's why I've seen how they arrive and leave to the group's backyard," Francisco finished his comment with a gesture of displeasure.

"The group's backyard?" asked Jackie with a surprised face. Jackie was about to hear the story about the place where they sent people who, for some reason for their bosses that didn't have an acceptable work performance and instead of firing them, they were sent to a more distant place so that they would take the decision to resign by themselves.

She listened attentively Francisco's stories, doubting on what he was saying in some moments. but at the same time seeing in his eyes that desperation that made her believe in his words.

Jackie took a good part of the morning in the first interview. Several hours the conversation lasted. There was a lot to do at the club. She had to know them and start working immediately in the summer course which was about to start. There was no time to lose, therefore when Francisco left her office she asked her assistant to find the other managers and arrange the interviews in the best possible way.

GO AHEAD WITH THE SUMMER COURSE!

Jackie finished her first interview very close to noon. Immediately after Francisco left, she asked Alexia to look for any background of past summer courses. She turned her gaze away and realized that there were several folders in a piece of furniture in the office. She approached to take one of them and began to review it.

In them she found documents about the soccer club history. There were newspaper and photo clippings stored in protective plastic. She remembered the hall just outside her office's entrance, where there were more framed photographs, all famous players of the team.

Alexia told her the story of each photo. They there were from the beginning, until the last championships won by the team. The whole place was filled with memories and old glories. They stopped to watch one of the photos where a one of the players on it was also one person working now in the club. It was Professor Erik, a great player who had been famous for being one of the best goalkeepers the team had.

The Professor was the soccer school director. The school received children from five to twelve years old. There were different categories, different coaches, but obviously because of his experience, Erik oversaw all the categories.

Alexia explained to Jackie the importance of talking to Erik about the summer course, thus the activity most children wanted was precisely soccer. In addition, it was necessary to consider that the getting all the children in through the main entrance of the club was impossible, so during a month, the entrance for the summer course was enabled by the soccer school facilities.

Jackie struggled not to think out loud, but clearly showed a worried face when she realized that there wasn't much time to organize that event. She thanked her assistant for the information and returned to her office.

A couple of minutes later, her thinking was interrupted by the sound of her telephone extension. It was Alexia, who told her she had found the sports manager and had told him to meet her after lunch. At the same time Alexia informed her that in her inbox was the information about the last summer courses. Alexia was a very good assistant, originally from the Highlands of Jalisco. She was discreet, pretty, and reliable.

Jackie decided to ask for some food from the cafeteria and eat in her office, during the lunch hours she checked the information of the last summer courses looking for a description of specific procedures, but instead she only found projections, incomplete working minutes. It was necessary to give them a system, a correct form, however she had a beginning now.

She took a blank sheet of paper and started writing what she considered important to know, as if her children were going to be in those courses. With the information she had received and with her questionnaire, she began to elaborate in a simple method what she named as the "Description of the Project."

The basic ideas Jackie began to develop were based on four main points:

1. The children's safety during the time they were in the club from their departure until they are delivered to their parents at the end of the day.

2. The different activities they would have to do within the course.

3. Nutrition

4. Fun

Jackie was certain children wanted to spend a nice time, the categories were the same than at the soccer school, so she had a big task, because the older the children, the harder it was to do something fun for them.

We already have something, as a mom who wants to take her children to a course like this, I've something already. but now I need to see it as a company. What benefits am I looking for in the club? Those were the thoughts Jackie had on how to build the project.

When Jackie started writing about the benefits for the club, she remembered the experiences from her past Directors. For example, Director Valverde, a temperamental and a few words man, who simply told her every area of a company should obtain a benefit and if there was no benefit within a project, it was not a project that was worth the effort. With that way of thinking, Jackie realized that each manager had to find their own benefit for this project. Presenting the benefits first would be much easier to provoke the commitment of all of them.

Jackie took the phone and told Alexia to call for all the managers the next day at nine a.m., to let them know the meeting would be to review the progress for the summer course. Just then, Jesus, the sports director arrived at the sitting area.

Alexia knocked softly at the door and entered the office while telling Jackie that Monreal was outside waiting to see her. Jackie asked her to wait a minute, just that she needed to keep all the documents and notes she had on her desk.

Jackie liked to interview people at the boardroom table she felt that an interview with a desk in between was not the right way to do it, sheset aside everything and went to receive him. "Come in Monreal, take a seat." Jackie pointed the chairs that were in front of her desk.

Jesus Monreal was a graduate with a degree in Physical Education and Sport. With Francisco, they were the managers who had most time working at the club. Jackie realized by the attitude of Monreal that something wasn't right, so she changed tactics with him and asked directly, "Well, Jesus let's start, but before that I would like to ask why you are so unconfutable?"

Monreal didn't expect that, for him that interview was a waste of time. He already had a lot on his plate, problems at home, the summer course is coming, and now he also had to go and talk with the new Director. "Look, Director, the truth is, I have a lot of work, so I ask you please tell me what you want to know? They're waiting for me at the sports office. I must interview the staff that's going to oversee the summer course groups and that takes a lot of time," said Monreal in a rushed tone.

Jackie felt in those moments the strongest blood flow in her head. With an annoyed face told him, "Okay, we can do it as easy or as difficult as you want Monreal." Jackie's voice became louder. "I don't understand, and to be honest I'm shocked. In lees than a week we begin with the summer course, and you still don't have your staff. In how many summer courses have you ever been on?" Jackie asked.

"Come on, Director! I've participated in every summer course. I've been responsible of the children's sports activities," answered Monreal with a proud voice tone.

"I'm glad to hear you've got experience, but then, why do you leave something as important as choosing the attendants for the groups for few days before starting?" Jackie questioned him directly. At that moment, one may have felt the tension in the room.

"For the simple and tiny reason that the human resources department can't finish the contracts on time. There's been times when the exact same day we're beginning the course, the personnel is signing their contracts. I know those are things I shouldn't say, but you'll realize how we work here at the backyard, but don't worry, you'll figure everything out by yourself, this club gets to be the last one in everything," said Jesus, complaining about the situation.

For Monreal, it was very difficult to hide the slowness with which things happened in the club. Most of the time you had to wait for several weeks to hire someone, all the paperwork and requirements that had to be covered even after selecting a person were a real torture.

"What do you mean with 'the backyard?'" Monreal began explaining why he referred the sports club like that. He gave more than one example of the things that had happened and why all those who worked there considered themselves "the outsiders" of the group. Jackie listened carefully to Monreal's stories, feeling during the chatting about working in a place where everybody considered him a disaster zone. There weren't much to say, only listen. They went fast from one topic to another. Jackie tried focusing in the summer course better, asked Monreal if at the following day meeting he could bring a general description of the activities planned to share with all the Directors.

THE MAGNIFICENT TWELVE REUINITED

Tuesday, nine o'clock in the morning. Jackie had arrived early. She had put blank sheets and pens for all the managers on the boardroom table. She was determined to make them work as a team. She'd spent a good part of the night thinking about the way of making the managers find by themselves at least one benefit from the project they were about to build together.

She had a good plan, she would start first with the women who had children, then she would pass to the set of activities listed by categories. For each proposal, it was essential to include one or several security measures, and at the end of the meeting she wanted to include the topic of nutrition and food. Jackie liked brainstorming a lot. She always used a blackboard or enabled a window to write each proposal. She had to take advantage of time to the maximum. Jackie had in mind most of the benefits that she'd found for each area and was very sure that by making them participate together they could find more information than they already had.

With a little desperation to start the meeting, she opened the boardroom door and listened to the murmur of people climbing the stairs. She looked at her assistant and together they welcomed such a scandalous group of people.

One by one they were occupying the seats inside the boardroom. After ten minutes almost, everyone was in the office except for Professor Erik Von Zinga. He began early a meeting at the stadium, so he'd join them later. There was a calm atmosphere yet. Jackie closed the door of the office and the meeting began.

For a few seconds everyone was silent. Jackie took the moment to get in the front seat and started asking if they knew why they were, that was something common for her to do, trying to break the ice and that was the way she chose to start, but then again, the silence continued, no one spoke or made any comment. Jackie got up from her chair and started writing the title of the meeting on the top of the board: "General plan for the summer course."

When she finished she expected a comment or something, but they all continued in silence, they'd just moved their heads around and saw each other faces. No one seemed interested in making any comment nor saying something related to the subject. "It seems that early morning meetings are not very attractive for anyone, right?" commented Jackie looking for some laughs. "Let's see, where are the moms of the group?" Five of the seven women raised their hands.

"We are going to do an exercise. If you, as moms, are looking for a summer course for your children, what would be the first thing you'll ask for the course to have so you'll consider signing them up?" asked Jackie.

Before any mother spoke or answer something, Jackie heard Camila's voice saying that she didn't have children, but if she had them she would never let them be in that club, less in this summer course. When she finished saying those comments, Camila looked for Jackie's eyes. She continued by saying, "To start the last time the we had a lot of complaints. The schools had to end up in returns, because they promised activities that were never done." She followed her speech saying that there had been also many accidents in the pool due to the poor condition of its tiles. "There are areas where just by touching the bottom can cause several wounds. As you know most of the facilities are old and lack of maintenance," she continued saying in a very reasonable tone. During this, all the managers crossed looks only to confirm what Camila was saying.

From the edge of the table Monreal was wanting to clarify that if there were activities that were not done was because they did not hire the staff he'd requested, because many of the guides were hired several days after already starting the course.

The eyes turned to Martha, the human resources manager, she turned her head to see Camila saying, "A certain 'someone' had forgotten to have on time the personnel requisition and if that wasn't enough, the requested pattern didn't match the budget they'd sent. In addition, it'd been necessary to include the new personnel that the sports area had requested, reason for which the permissions were released a few days after having started the course."

From one moment to the next, everyone in that place was already talking, Jackie was recognizing the way they react. She'd heard many times while styling her Masters, "You cannot move forward in any situation without having confronted what motivated it." Learning how work teams feel and think is a challenge for the person in charge. What was going on in the board room was a confrontation.

Jackie let each one expose what they thought of that project. In her mind she tried desperately to memorize what each of them had done. She didn't want to lose the continuity of things. What she wanted was for the team to realize things that caused all those bad results. "How about if we start writing on the board how all that happened?" she requested. I would like to know what triggered that avalanche of problems.

Jackie hadn't finished speaking, when Camila got up from her seat and with a very loud and paused voice began telling them the way she thought and felt. "You really want to know what's going on around here?" Camila said looking especially at Jackie. "We all know what's happening, but no one dares to say it. Everything's wrong at this place. The club is located miles away from everything, the place itself is horrifying, nobody is engaged to your jobs, you're all a bunch of hypocrites." Camila's eyes seem so lit. She looked at them with a deep desperation. "I feel that everything that they said about this club is true, every single person refers to this place as "the worst of the worse." Camila finished expressing what they all knew, but no one dares to accept.

When Camila finished what she determined was her reality, Jackie visibly dismayed tried to answer, "I had it with you! You all feel disregard for the club, I haven't found a single person who wants to be here. Each one of you should be grateful for having a job and the only thing I find are irritated faces and a sea full of disappointments." Jackie's eyes began to fill up with tears, she ducked her head and looked for a tissue in her purse. Watching Jackie losing control like that was very uncomfortable.

At that moment Camila got up from the chair again and immediately raised her voice saying, "Oh honey, it appears that things here are making you lose control, and I don' t have time nor desire for your crying. So, when you feel better and understand the reality we can continue." After saying those strong words, Camila took her things and left in a hurry.

Jackie was struggling to remove the tears on her face while starting to say, "I think it's time to go and have breakfast, what do you think if we change the meeting for later?" Trying not to cry when talking. At that time everyone began to collect their belongings and leave the meeting room quickly. Jackie's efforts to maintain tranquility were evident. They had numerous "situations to solve" as she liked to call them.

Where's my coach now telling me to face the situation. She began to speak to herself in lonesome. Everything will be fine, she would constantly repeat herself alone in the place. But I want to know how we're going to face this project when the team is immobile without any sort of motivation or life. She kept thinking and talking to herself about finding a way to improve things. "To face" is, to speak face to face about what you feel and think of a situation that causes you exasperation or annoyance.

CONFRONTING REALITY

Jackie felt the need to search for Camila. What had happened that morning was uncomfortable for everyone, but the one who takes the first step is either exposed to being frowned upon or perhaps admired. Everything depends on the way you want to visualize it.

At that moment for the team, Camila was their voice, the voice that detected what was happening, admitted it with enough courage, and it was more than obvious that they needed to be corrected.

Jackie took the phone and tried to communicate with Camila, she wanted to go and face her, there was no need to was teany more time she needed to act immediately. When something in our thinking or environment is different from what we expected to happen, the first reaction is to confront. It is very difficult to speak about what you feel or think when the emotional charge pushes us against something or someone. It is very important to realize this situation because in those moments instead of facing, we could change the action and just push ourselves only to confront.

Confronting is a reaction that provokes an attitude of opposition within a situation that needs to be solved. The sound of the phone was heard in Camila's office over and over, but no one answered. She took her bag and left, determined to face the situation. It was visible the emotional weight Jackie felt, there was much concern in her due to Camila's comments.

While leaving her office, her assistant reminded her that she had an appointment. She hadn't met the owner of the restaurant and the cafeteria of the club. Jackie had to go and eat without being hungry. "Thanks Alexia, you're right I'd forgot. It seems I'll have to postpone my conversation with Camila." In Jackie's thoughts remained the pending confrontation. She knew she had to face it in another moment when she was calmer, still she continued to carry the unpleasant emotions Camila had caused.

With her mind full of cases to deal with, Jackie went to the restaurant. She'd to go through the soccer fields and the restaurant was surrounded by them. When she arrived at the place, the owner, Giovanni Maranello was already waiting for her. His greeting was a mixture of informality and warmth, but the smile he offered to Jackie had not been reflected the same way with the other Directors of the club

They immediately started a walk through the restaurant, Giovanni took her to the kitchen, where all the dishes were prepared. At that moment all the ingredients to cook the famous grilled fish were out, which, due to its flavor, was one of the specialties of the place.

When Jackie stopped in front of the vitrine that contained the fish, Giovanni approached her to explain the importance of fish in that dish, "When you want to surprise yourself with a different flavor, you must use a very fresh fish, in addition to having the best ingredients so that the final result is a real pleasure to your senses. Look, Jackie! look at these fish, do not get too close because they are so fresh that possibly some can flirt and move for you to take it," he ended up joking.

The supplier of the restaurant fish twice a week and it arrived in conditioned boxes to keep it truly fresh. Jackie was surprised, turned her head to look at Giovanni and with a doubtful expression dared to ask him, "So, these fish that you have here are alive?"

Giovanni replied, "Jackie, this fish is so fresh, that if we put any in the pool, it would surely be swimming with all those people." She showed a gesture of disbelief, although the fish had the appearance of being alive, therefore she didn't know if Giovanni has joking again or speaking seriously. "Jackie look at the eyes of the fish, they are bright! Fish, through their eyes show for how long it's been out of the sea. Despite being immobile its eyes continue having that brightness that makes you confused." Giovanni took two fish and put them on a special plate, at that point he directed Jackie to a table, asked her to choose one of them, so they would cook it at that moment.

Jackie was thoughtful, she had been staggered by Giovanni's comments about the fish, so she asked him to choose the best one, and attending to her petition, Giovanni took the one with the brightest eyes, handed it to the waiter to take him to the kitchen asking him to cook it with the house's special flavor.

Giovanni got up, walked a few steps towards the bar, took two bottles of water, cleaned them and returned. Kindly smiled at Jackie and asked her to choose one of the bottles, the one she thought was fresher.

Jackie opened her eyes widely and answered instantly that just by looking at the bottles she couldn't know which would be fresher, she had to feel them to know which of the two was the correct one. Giovanni then began telling her what his father had told him when they went fishing for the first time. "It was the first and last time that I went fishing with my old man. I was seven, and the emotion of watching how fish were taken out of the water with those nets and storage in a container with water and I'll never forget that. My father told me there wasn't enough space to keep so much fish. I'd to choose which were coming with us, and which were going back to the ocean.

"The bucket we had in the boat was big and I could see how there was some fish fighting to get out and return to the sea, but there were also a few who were immobile, those were at the bottom, giving the appearance of being already defeated.

"In those times, Jackie, next to my father, I learned that I should feel with the gaze and simply help those fish that jumped and struggled to return to the sea," Giovanni finished telling his experience.

"What a situation Giovanni! Jackie replied very aware of everything," she'd shared with her new friend. "But tell me why you decided to take out those fish that jumped and moved? If I'd been you, I would have kept those fish that were full of energy," said Jackie with a gaze of wonder.

Giovanni took one of the bottles of water on the table, took a sip and continued the conversation. "I'll explain what I learned that day without realizing it. The fish that are in the bottom, without moving are bigger, and I do not say that they're big in size, they're bigger in meat, in their volume. the weight of their meat doesn't allow them to jump the same way as the youngest fish, those leaps are hardly in development, the taste of its meat is not as delicious as that of a bigger and mature fish." Just in that minute, their conversation was interrupted by the smell of the fish that was being cooked. That smell, so different, so fascinating. In Jackie's eyes you could see her impatience for trying out the fish.

Jackie had a blend of sensations because Giovanni's story made a lot of sense. Giovanni excused himself from the table and went on to check how the dishes were going. Jackie used that moment to get her ideas in order. She was barely understanding the fish-in-glass syndrome when, from one moment to the next, she struggled to understand the meaning of feeling with her gaze. Jackie was again talking out loud, this time imagining the things she'd talked with Giovanni, and her laughter started to be heard all over the place.

Giovanni came out of the kitchen with a bottle of white wine and two glasses. Without asking anything he served both, gave Jackie one of them and asked her the reason of her smile. The blushing on her face was surprising. She told him that she was simply imagining herself inside the bucket trying to leave and come back to the ocean.

"Why did you imagine that Jackie?" Giovanni asked her with a very interested expression.

"I'm going to trust in you and tell you the reason," Jackie said, having a taste from her glass of wine. "When I stayed in front of the fish vitrine, and you told me that. If we throw the fish to the pool they could swim again. You really made me doubt, the same way I doubted while I was talking to my team a few hours ago. I imagined them as the fish inside the vitrine, they were there with their bright eyes open, but their minds were elsewhere."

Giovanni's laugh also was perceived, now, it was him who was naming every fish under the glass. He told her, she was right, that in fact some fish had a slightly similar look to them.

Jackie continued her explanation, "After you told me about the fish inside the bucket, I imagined myself next to my Directors right inside of it. I'm jumping and trying to find my way back to the sea or trying to find my way out of this place." Now, both laughed even harder, and some diners around them were laughing with them too without even knowing why.

In that second someone with a huge plate came out of the kitchen, there it was, the famous "grilled fish." One side of the plate had a red berries salad, and on the other an exquisite snow-covered rice.

Jackie changed her laughter for a staggered expression. She'd never tasted that dish, in fact she didn't like a whole fish on her plate. She said the spines made her waste a lot of time and when she removed them they made her clean her hands many times to remove the smell on her fingers.

As if Giovanni knew what she was thinking, he held two forks and skillfully separated the meat of the fish almost instantaneously and served Jackie a portion of each food that was in the big plate. "Thank you very much Giovanni, how did you know that I don't like to remove the spines of these little animals?" Jackie said, pointing fingers pointing to the fish in front of her.

Giovanni's laughter came again. "Let me tell you that I didn't like to be separating spine by spine, but my mother taught me how to discover the meat without touching the fishes' backbone at all," Giovanni said showing her again how to do it, he was serving himself a similar portion to the one he'd given to Jackie.

When she cut a piece of meat from the fish and put it in her mouth, she could see why that dish was the specialty of the place. "Dear, God! What a delight! This special taste. I had never tasted something similar before, but tell me Giovanni, you know how to cook this delight?" asked Jackie.

"I'm going to tell you a secret Jackie," Giovanni whispered. "My family comes from a small town in Italy where men go fishing and women stay at home preparing everything for the time the grill and each ingredient is ready for cooking when they have what the ocean dares to give us. All the ingredients for this dish are important, but, there's one that makes the complete difference: the grilling. I'm an only child, and my mother spoiled me a lot, so, she convinced my father to let me stay at home with her and learn the secrets of her cooking. With time and due to my sea sickness when I got into a boat or any other type of structure that moves in the sea, I had to learn the secrets di mia mama. To me, it was always hard to accept that my dad was a fisherman and I couldn't get in a boat without getting sick and green from the motion." Laughter between both increased, when Giovanni told Jackie that now he was picturing himself inside the same bucket as a fish jumping to return to land rather than the ocean.

The fish was about to end, and the talking was very pleasant, nevertheless it was time to return to the office, the time Jackie had arranged to go to eat without hunger, she had left many things to think about. "What's up Jackie? Why that look? Perhaps you don't know that the best is yet to come," said Giovanni. Without saying anything else, one of the waiters approached the table with different types of desserts. All of them looked quite appetizing. Giovanni recommended the strawberry tart, it was made with a recipe from his grandmother. Jackie accepted the dessert and with that delight in front of her, she understood why Giovanni had told her that the best was yet to come.

"Always the sweetest comes at the end," thought Jackie. In the meantime, she turned her eyes to the soccer field, and at that moment a group of children were about to begin the training, which, with great excitement, disturbed the tranquility that existed in the environment.

THE RED DRAGONS INVADE THE FIELD

Almost immediately a group of people, children, and adults surrounded the soccer court completely that same field that minutes ago was totally empty could feel an environment of expectation. Everybody wanted to see that group of children's training.

"Who are those children? They're making a good fuss. it seems to me that they're all playing and laughing, you can feel they're having fun," pondered Jackie.

"That's it Jackie, you're feeling with your gaze. That group of children as you called them are this club representative team. They are 'the Little Dragons.' As you can see there are many people who come see them train. I think you don't know it but from that team have come incredible players like "the ejotito." Today those players are playing for recognized international teams," Giovanni explained proudly.

"I don't like that sport. I've never been in a soccer match nor in any real stadium for that matter," commented Jackie, with a slight bush on her cheeks.

"Well, you're going to learn a lot of things about soccer here. You know you're joining me right now, let's go to the field. I'm introducing you to Professor Erik since he's the soccer school manager and that team's coach." Without giving her a chance to refuse, Giovanni got up from the table and headed towards the side entrance of the pitch. When they took the first steps there, Jackie felt under her shoes the thickness of the grass. It seems as if she walked under a quite thick rug. Then, Jackie got chilled, she didn't want to continue walking in that place. She felt her high heels would damage the field. She could only walk a few steps and was planted as a statue at the edge of the pitch.

In the distance she saw Professor Erik's silhouette, who noticed Giovanni and Jackie's presence and caught up with them quickly. "What a pleasant surprise, Director!" were Professor Erik's words to Jackie. At the same time, he greeted her with a kiss on the cheek and a warm hug. "I didn't have the pleasure of meeting you, but I've heard lots of comments about your arrival," said Professor Erik.

Prof Erik was a nice guy. He came from Anglo-Saxon origins. His full name is Erik Hammer Von Zinga. His father was German and his mother British. Being the only child of the Hammer Von Zinga marriage, Erik had always managed to stand out for his attitude, but specially for making people's abilities to come out and shine. That special thing about him made him distinct anywhere he was.

After his retirement as a professional soccer player, he became a trainer for the club's basic forces. Thanks to his experience, he managed to form several championship teams in children's leagues. Now, despite having received different proposals to train professional teams, the Professor was still responsible of the soccer school and as the Little Dragons' coach.

"I only hope that those things have been good comments Professor. This club has been like an emotional roller coaster for me and I still haven't finished learning the place and all its members. Jackie replied with that smile that characterized her.

"But of course, they were all good comments Director. In fact, allow me to offer an apology. I was unable to get to the meeting I had scheduled with you for this morning. When I am in the stadium there is a bunch of things that must be done Time and distances do not help much in this city," Erik said.

"Yes, I understand perfectly Professor, don't worry. Let me tell you that we had to postpone the meeting. Camila was kind enough to share with me all her feelings saved inside her, feelings regarding the club, and I have to say, I didn't like the things she said. For that reason, we couldn't continue. But, how nice that we are talking now, because as you know the meeting is to define the strategic plan for the summer course that is just around the corner."

Professor Von Zynga's ragged laugh was inevitable, he knew Camila and knew this woman couldn't mince her words. Her strong appeal was already known by everyone.

The summer course is a very important event for the club. In countless occasions there were children who were waiting for their turn to get in specially because of the soccer courses. "To be honest Professor, I'm nervous to receive more than five hundred children next week," explained Jackie with horror in her face.

"Nervous, Director? Every time we start courses I always enjoy them. The entire soccer school is jam-packed, coaches in all the categories have their courses to the maximum, the visitors are triplicated, there are children of all ages," Erik argued with hand movements that showed great emotion for the event.

"Dear Lord! How is that? You really enjoy all of it? Now I'm beginning to feel more anguish than nerves. There are so many things to prepare and my managers are still unable to work as a team," explained Jackie. "Right at lunch with Giovanni we were talking about the fish in-glass syndrome, it seems as if everyone were sitting next to each other, with bright eyes wide open but without any movement." Again, the laughter of the three was inevitable.

Jackie's personality had done its thing, and without a doubt in a short time there was a connection made. Jackie looked around and saw how the children were doing their training between laughs and fun. A sign from Professor Von Zinga was enough to change exercises and the whole team moved at the same pace.

"It's amazing to see how the whole team is so integrated, I can even feel the children's smile at a distance, they are having so much fun, so many people around them, watching them and they keep running and juggling the ball, as if they didn't care about all the fuss they cause," Commented Jackie. "But, tell me Professor, what do you really do? How did you manage to make those little ones work as a team in that way?" Jackie's eyes went straight to Erik's. She wanted to know what they were doing in that team.

"Director, relax, the first thing you should do is calm down," Erik said in a low voice. "When one has a hectic mind, one cannot feel one's emotions. What you are feeling with the gaze is not their smile, it is the strength of their energy and the result of their teamwork. Those kids have known each other since they entered this school," explained the Professor, trying to get Jackie to understand why she felt that way.

Giovanni was their coach in the first category, after evolving, they entered the basic forces, from there until today Professor Erik has been their coach. Giovanni was also a professional player and disciple of Professor Hammer Von Zinga. He had an injury that led him to lose most of his career, but because of his restaurant experience he won the tender to offer and sell food at the club, with Erik's support, also he managed to coach in the soccer school at the same time

"All those children that you see at that field, all of them, no exceptions, share one single emotion. They feel so proud of being the Little Dragons," Professor Von Zinga finished explaining. The most prestigious children's soccer team in the city and with the highest number of championships gained, is precisely that group of kids who look so amused and caused so much fuss and excitement in the club. "Excuse me for not being able to continue with you. I must accompany my dragons in their training, but tomorrow morning if you want we couldmeet, and I will gladly tell you a little more about this. Let's put some background on the table, define things, let's make the Director no longer nervous to receive so much energy from the children that we will have in the course." Among laughter he said goodbye to both, Giovanni and Jackie, and jogged intothe training, for Jackie it had been a pleasant afternoon, there were many things to think about.

Jackie and Giovanni were watching a little more of that team's training, they could watch as each group does different exercises. In front of each of them was a little dragon, a member of the team that set the example on how to do things, spent a few minutes there and changed exercise, but also helped as a leader. One by one all the Little Dragons were going to the front. Each one of them had to show a movement to follow the training.

When Jackie realized what they were doing, she remembered the way geese flocks fly south in cold weather. Nature is our best teacher and always has a lot to teach us. The way geese travel enormous distances without stopping, is a convincing proof of that. These flocks use a" V" formation to perform their act. As each bird flits its wings generates an air stream, which elves and helps the goose that comes from behind achieving distances far greater than what each would fly on its own. As soon as a goose goes out of formation feels the drag and the resistance of the air because of flying alone, it returns immediately integrating itself to the formation again, which means that it naturally learns the advantages of group flight. When the guide goose gets tired, it takes in rotation its position at the tail of the formation and the next goose takes its place. Each goose of the flock knows perfectly where it is going and the speed that its flight must have. Jackie had heard many times that form of collaboration that geese have, but never observed the same in a group of people.

In this team formed by dragons, they took advantage of each step, the advantages of working together they know it was easier to prepare with the support and confidence of all its members. Dragons, like geese, have a sense of belonging to a group, that makes everyone in the team prepare and train to properly perform every activity that ties them to the game.

There were occasions that, for some reason a dragon isn't in the mood to train or maybe due to illness could not play a soccer match, then some member of the team joins the partner who couldn't be present until he returned to the team again. This type of action causes each group member to be always present when necessary and help the other in their quick recovery.

"Giovanni, thank you very much for the food, it was delicious, but above all thank you for sharing your stories with me." It was time to go back to the office, Jackie had many things to solve, so she shook Giovanni's hand as a gesture of kindness.

AN AFTERNOON OF TWISTED FISH

Jackie was heading back to her office, in her thoughts was only the way of making the managers' team to respond. It was time to return the fish to the sea, so they could be real fish again and we could see them swim all around. How can I take that disparagement feeling out? How can I make them feel the excitement of working in a team? How can I turn this "backyard" into a different place? A place where everyone wants to be at. So many questions, and so little time, things needed to be done. Jackie was submerged in her thoughts with all those questions, when suddenly she saw someone arriving to her office. In her office's waiting room was Martha sited with her legs crossed.

When they were face to face, Jackie stopped for a moment to tell her in a very kind voice, "It's so nice to see you Martha!" Martha's look seemed impatient. She wanted to finish with that unpleasant feeling that had gotten her to that place once and for all. Without saying a word, she rose from the sofa and got in Jackie's office. Jackie let Martha enter, saw a different expression on her face and immediately gave instructions to her assistant, "Alexia let no one interrupt us." Jackie closed the door and directed her attention to Martha, invited her to take a seat, and started preparing two cups of tea in the kitchenette. Those seconds in silence, caused that visitor's breath to accelerate.

Visibly altered Martha managed to sketch a ragged phrase, "Jackie, I don't want to take waste much of your time, I just come to tell you that...I resign!" Martha's voice was very fragile when talking to Jackie. "I feel that I don't belong to this place," Martha continued nervously.

From the kitchenette, Jackie turned to see her pretending not to give importance to what she had heard, asking her, "Sugar, Martha?" Jackie approached her giving her a cup and two envelopes of sugar, took a seat next to her and with a curious voice asked her, "In which part of the group did you said you worked before? "

The expression on Martha's face was puzzled but little by little she began to relax. "At the human resources department. I was responsible of providing the rest of the areas the necessary people for the correct function and operation of the place." Martha's voice sounded way calmer.

"And, how did you feel there?" Jackie kept questioning.

"Well, I had my office in the stadium, I was always pressured, I mean, always trying to find the right people to operate each department correctly. But generally, I felt ok. I think I did a good job!" Martha replied.

"You think you did a good job? Why did you think that Martha?" asked Jackie looking directly into her eyes.

Martha relaxed her shoulders and kept talking about everything she had done before, how she had to look for the best people, and remembered the way in which, despite all sorts of limitations, she felt she fulfilled her responsibilities. Although it was true that there were no correct indicators to measure Martha's work, nevertheless she knew with precision what things she had to do to feel that she was doing a good job. The conversation continued with much more confidence between both.

"Now Martha, in the same way that you're telling me what you did before, I would like you to tell me, why do you feel that you don't belong in this place?" Jackie said, pulling back a little and getting comfortable in her chair. Jackie was getting ready to receive any amount of comments from her, but instead Martha began speaking in a much quieter way, showing a more relaxed expression.

"I feel that most of my colleagues come to work forcibly. I think they are only surviving in this place. Some have been around for a long time, and many others have arrived but in less than a month they've resigned," Martha continued to speak with disappointment on her face. Martha had been working in the club for more than a year and since the day she arrived she'd been told that things were going to change. That the place would be a model for similar clubs. But, things she'd lived there had disappointed her a lot.

Both turned their eyes into each other, they knew there was something there that wasn't working correctly. Martha feared to make Jackie have another jolt, but despite of that, she wanted to vent all that she had carried during the time spent in that club. "And you Martha? What's the motivation that make you come to work? Why haven't you left?" When Martha listened to those questions turned her eyes down. It can be felt just by looking at her. She was struggling to find the answer inside her. "Why have you waited so long for running out of here? Why are you still here? Most people come to work forcibly so I would like to know, why are you still here?" Jackie restricted herself looking for answers, while Martha's mind began a quick search for arguments that would justify continuing in that toxic place. Jackie got up from the chair at last and approached the board where she wrote the word "Emotion."

To continue, she looked at Martha and kept writing words to help her explain that concept: An emotion is a reaction which makes one act in a certain way, your personality is a filter that makes the intensity in which one's feeling increases or decreases. Our life is filled with emotions, from the moment we're inside our mother's womb we can feel them.

In those moments Jackie spoke and stared at Martha's eyes for continuing sharing her thoughts. Jackie ought to convey to Martha what she had learned about the subject. She knew that during the passage through any public or private school or university, those concepts were not important to anyone and Martha was the most emotional person inher team, so she kept writing about it. These reactions are used to establish our position regarding the place where we are and what we perceive with our senses. It was the second paragraph that Jackie was writing on the blackboard. When she finished she sat next to Martha again.

"When you started telling me what you felt and thought, I began to perceive a feeling of despair on your part towards all your colleagues. When you told me a few moments ago that you were giving up and resigning, you took me by surprise," continued Jackie explaining to Martha.

"You are right Jackie, many times I have wanted to run out of this place, I'm very desperate. There have been many events that make me feel exhausted. I no longer feel the excitement of working for the best soccer team in the country." Martha started talking, trying to understand why she reacted in that way. "When I arrived at the club I had many ideas, but little by little I was just saving them, when I realized how things are done here. You know something Jackie, I want to study a master's in Spain. The group has offices there, I'm very enthused to think that I can work in Barcelona." Martha continued to talk without showing too much emotion or lack of control and without losing eye contact with Jackie. Martha went from one emotion to another. she encouraged herself to talk about her plans. but later she lost interest when she realized what she was doing at that moment.

"Martha it's great that you want to study a master's, I assure you that at the beginning it will be a bit difficult, but you should not give up on your dreams. I, just like you, have gone through many different sensations in making things happen here. Sometimes at night I find it hard to fall asleep, I'm just thinking about finding the best way to build a different sports club. A place where everyone wants to be!" Jackie knew she couldn't do it alone, and realizing how things were happening, I was going to need all the help possible. So, she kept talking to Martha.

"No Jackie, that enthusiasm that you say doesn't work in here. That has caused me for everyone to see me as the club weeper, but I cannot continue, I'll just wait until the end of the month and I'll give you everything that corresponds to my position. I give up!" said Martha sharply, and turning around left the office leaving Jackie perplexed. What things had to happen to start with that emotional burden? What caused her to feel that she does not belong to this club. A feeling is the result of emotions. In Martha's case there must have been many unpleasant emotions. to make her feel that she should not continue in the club. One feeling at a time and you would enjoy each emotion to the maximum. Maybe when there's an unpleasant feeling too ingrained towards something or someone, the best thing would be to move it away so that it does not contaminate the rest of the members of the team. But, it seems everybody has the same feeling? One way or another, they're all upset and annoyed with the club. They show anger and sadness for feeling relegated towards the club, you can't stay without staff in the group. Thought Jackie.

Right there with all her emotions still exposed, Jackie decided to write in her notepad all the answers that were emerging in her mind, even if she didn't have any resolution to them now, nonetheless by writing them she felt that at any time she could find the answer.

"But, then, how can I achieve making people do what they must do wanting?" were the first words Jackie wrote down. After a few seconds, she wrote: "And, would they know what they want to do? It seems no one wants to do anything, the fish in-glass syndrome is spreading like an epidemic disease." Jackie was concentrated in finding the form to build a sports club where everyone wanted to be at. In the little time she'd been working at the club, she's noticed the different stages that her work team was facing. She had to find as accurately and quickly as possible a solution for what was happening. She knew how to apply different study tools to know the internal and external situation of a company, dominated the traditional way of making a business diagnosis. "But how to identify what they need?" Jackie had always said joking that she was a business doctor. She'd had a huge number of patients in her hands. She had become an expert in diagnosing business illnesses. She had the necessity to use a business scanner to detect possible corporate illnesses.

Then again, in this case and to her great surprise in her hands was a patient with a rare disease. In Jackie's mind this patient could not wait. That epidemic illness that was attacking the club was proceeding very fast, she had to act quickly.

That night when going upstairs to enter her apartment Jackie felt the excessive weight in her calves, that accumulation of ambiances that made her feel tired, and very exhausted. For her, this new adventure made her feel all kinds of emotions that kept her in a permanent state of alertness. She could identify what was necessary to find the cure for her group

A CUP OF COFFEE WITH A DIFFERENT FLAVOR

Jackie was getting into the club's parking lot almost an hour before her entry time. She was searching different roads to get to work with the less setbacks as possible, she had to look for several routes to avoid traffic as much as possible. In a huge city like that, traffic jams, car accidents and things like that were an everyday thing. In that occasion the road from her house to the club has been considerable quick. Jackie felt content and rested above all. She could sleep pleasingly.

She finished parking her car and decided to find the most convenient way to get to her office when she met Professor Von Zinga, both had arrived at the same time. "Good morning Jackie, what are you doing here this early?" Professor Erik asked with a curious tone.

"Professor Erik, good morning to you too. You know, I've always had the habit of arriving before working hours, I like to enjoy a good cup of coffee peacefully before starting activities," Jackie said with an air of calmness in her expressions.

"What great habits Jackie, unfortunately I cannot share the last of them. But I just had a great idea, come with me, I'm going to take you to a place where you could always have a cup of freshly roasted coffee. Besides, those people have something they share with you." Von Zinga finished speaking and took Jackie by the arm and started to walk together towards the most isolated part of the club.

During the walk Erik was talking to Jackie about the place where he would take her. The Professor had noticed some uncertainty on her, but also curiosity to know what it was. They kept walking and entered the soccer school oldest facilities. They had to go to that place, where there was a large jacuzzi, which a certain group of people used very early every day. When Jackie listened to the professor's explanation and observed the place they were entering, she felt instantaneously different things that made her doubt whether to continue or not. Erick kept telling her the story of that site, explaining the way in which it had been used.

The upper part of the building was in a 40-room area, before losing its charm the rooms were used as concentration quarters for the team's starting lineup players. If a match was held on a Sunday, the players were gathered in those quarters at least three days before the match, continued their training so that on the day of the game three hours before the game they could all leave together for the stadium. In those moments they were crossing the same rooms that Erik was describing. "So, tell me Professor what happened then? Because now you can perceive an atmosphere of abandonment in this whole place," Jackie interrupted with amazement for what she was listening to.

"That is a fine question Jackie! Professor Erik stopped to answer." He saw clearly in Jackie's eyes the desperation to discover the causes that had led to that situation. "You do not have to be an architect to realize that in most part of the facilities of the whole club you get a sense of abandonment and total neglect."

"Every time I listen to someone who works or is a member in the club, they make me feel the same," said Jackie with kind of impatiently.

Professor Erik continued, "When we met at the entrance a few minutes ago you told me about some habits you have before starting work. You told me that you are here this early, so you could calmly enjoy a good cup of coffee and that's something important for you. There you have the explanation Jackie. The answer is in what you said. The sum of those habits makes the difference," explained Erik while rotating his wrist, seeking to refer to those people that Jackie was referring to.

"I don't understand Professor, what does my habits have to do with the perception of abandonment that this place makes me feel," questioned Jackie.

"Do not worry Jackie, in a moment I assure you, you will understand easier what I am trying to explain," said the Professor.

They followed their trajectory to the end of those rooms, Jackie had an expression of disbelief, in her mind she was still looking for that relationship that Professor Von Zinga wanted to make her understand.

They reached the last door and with a big pull of the knob they managed to open it. "Here we are Jackie, come in please," indicated Erik. When they opened the door, the first thing one observed was a big white wall, and a small table in the middle. There were different plates with fruit. Also, there two aluminum pitchers. In one of them, the coffee Erik had promised Jackie.

"Come in Jackie, help yourself! This pitcher contains the roasted coffee and this one here has hot water with a slightly taste of mint if you are in the mood for a delicious tea. That is what I have the habit to drink every morning," explained the Professor.

Jackie took one of the mugs located on a bar and quickly served coffee in it without adding any sugar. "No sugar Jackie?" Erik asked.

"That's right Professor, no sugar, for me, coffee must be drunk without sugar, just like that it's the way you can enjoy its aroma and everything you can feel when you take the first sip," answered Jackie while she smelled her drink.

The atmosphere inside that room full of humidity, was visible the steam that detached from the following windows, that made that place different. "Behind this wall, there are glass doors separating the wet area from the main room. what you see now is made by a group of people who have the habit of getting together every morning. They bring fruit and everything you can taste here. As you can tell, this room is different from the others we went before, the perception that you are forming from this will be different when you meet the elderly people who have this habit." Jackie was stupefied by Erik's words, she would never have imagined that those who used that old jacuzzi would be older people. "They meet here to do something very similar to what you do when drinking coffee with no sugar. They manage to enjoy the moment, leaving aside the things that could make those moments less pleasant." Once again, the surprised Jackie's face appeared. "All of them leave aside the thought of being in a deteriorated place and just enjoy what they get from a nice bath and a decent breakfast. You would be surprised to see how many the times they get in the jacuzzi in the same morning. All those people let their feelings appreciate each moment, everything they are living." Professor Von Zinga looked at Jackie directly, he tried to explain her in a diverse form, the reason for thinking about that older people's group, and the importance of living each day to the fullest. "When you get to certain age, you realize you spent most of your life letting one situation or another takes control not allowing you to have peace and tranquility to savor every moment and thing you are facing."

"Such weird costumes this people have Professor!" Jackie exclaimed. "I've always heard that if you take a hot bath you wouldn't go outside right away."

"It's not a costume Jackie, they have a habit," the Professor was telling her. "Costumes are determined by a nation's ideas or a particular group. Costumes are general and accepted.

Habits are individual and learned. They are unique to learn and acquire. They are determined by our own ideas, feelings and experiences. There are positive habits and negative habits as well. The same thing happens with costumes. This that can be important for one person, maybe in a different community or a different country could be offensive. It all depends in the way you see it. The perception you get inside you towards what you do or have as a costume and as a habit. Most people have listened that same thing you've just said Jackie, people say you could catch a cold if you go outside when you have just taken a shower or bath," explained Von Zinga. "Having a perception of what others say has become a costume in our lives. For that reason, a lot of times we perceive situations that are like what others say, nevertheless they are a little or a lot far from reality. For instance, what you think Jackie, about taking a hot bath early and then getting outside of the house right after," kept explaining Erik. "I assure you that the same happens when people talk negatively about this club, many of them get carried away by what they hear from others and have a different perception of reality. I cannot deny that there are many things to improve here, but that does not mean that everything in the club is bad or has a total carelessness as you asked me Jackie." Professor Von Zinga paused after these comments and began to prepare his usual cup of tea.

Jackie was learning to understand the difference between habit and costume. There are some habits that can help us break certain costumes, and of course Jackie was thinking about all the things that she saw differently. The way in which each person constructs the physical reality of what he or she observes, and feels is known as perception. The habit of perceiving things through sensations received by other people is something we should stop doing. Creating the habit of facing circumstances that need to be solved with a neutral perception will allow us to have a broad and objective vision of the reality that we are facing.

"What do you think about the coffee that these people are inviting us Jackie?" The professor interrupted Jackie's thoughts with his question.

"You're absolutely right, this coffee has a different flavor." Answered Jackie with a smile on her face.

"By the way Jackie, Giovanni has asked me to let you know that today at lunch time, he will prepare a special dish to welcome you to the club. The soccer school has the pleasure of inviting you and your entire managers team to join us this evening at the restaurant," Von Zinga finished the invitation very diplomatically.

"Professor, one more surprise. I'm very grateful to you two. Yesterday when I met Giovanni, I believed he was a very nice person, I realize you both share the way of seeing life. between you two have made everything I have to solve be more bearable. Yesterday was complicated, Martha came to my office and presented her resignation, we have little time to define the action plan for the summer course. I would like to thank both, Giovanni and you, but it seems to me that on this occasion I will not be able to join you," Jackie apologized kindly.

"Well, it will be a bit strange not to have you at your welcome lunch, since yesterday we have notified everyone, and we are preparing the necessary so that our habit of harmony does not break." The joke tone the Professor used to convince Jackie was very evident. and the laughter that provoked that was spontaneous.

"Well, if it's about continuing with a good habit, who am I to break it?" Answered Jackie laughing and finally accepting the invitation.

THE WELCOME MEAL

After the coffee with Professor Erik, Jackie remained the whole morning locked in her office writing on the board and filling it with notes. She wrote things on her pad too. She was looking for the best way to break with the customs that were in the club. She was sure there were good things, you just had to discover them.

It was two o'clock in the afternoon and everyone was already in the restaurant. The delicious smell Jackie knew the day before was in the air again. Giovanni urged a table near a soccer field. The sight they had made them feel that they had in fronta huge garden in front of them.

The table was served, there was no need to wait for anyone else, the meal had started. Each of the guests began enjoying the dishes, there were two waiters who were always smiling, removing and putting plates as needed. The Professor was sitting next to Jackie. Everyone was enjoying the show and it seemed like everything was quiet.

"Good thing they accepted our invitation Director! I see the whole team is relaxed," Professor Von Zinga commented, with a trace of bread in the corner of his mouth.

"Yes Professor, yesterday was hectic and I hope today will define the key points for the summer course more clearly," commented Jackie.

"Let me tell you what arrived!" Exclaimed Erik very excited. "The new uniforms finally arrived, now they come with short pants and a jersey. We are going to be able to present them during the summer course, they are very similar to used by the leading team. you will see director." Jackie had no idea what effect of belonging to a professional soccer team could cause on people.

That same day but hours before, right in front of the Club's entry Jackie was driving and she made a prohibited turn and an officer was in the place. Immediately asked her to stop. Jackie, embarrassed by the mistake, stopped the vehicle and unconsciously started looking for her license in her handbag.

"Morning Miss, you just committed a traffic offense. Please allow me your documents. Tell me, where are you going in such a hurry?" The officer with an authoritative voice questioned her.

"Good day official, I'm going to work, I work at the club that is right in front of us. I have a very important meeting today," Jackie pointed to the club's entrance. "I know, it is not an excuse, but I didn't realize that it was forbidden to turn here, give me a moment to find my license. The truth is that I have an important meeting and it was easier for me to turn left here than to go all the way to the roundabout." Jackie was justifying what she'd done at the same time she kept looking for her license. And thinking she must have forgotten it at the stadium, she remembered at that moment when she did not find anything in the purse.

"Look, officer let's do something, could you give me the ticket? I've been very stressed, and I surely leave my license at the stadium. As I already told you I have an important meeting with the other managers of the club and I can't be late," she finished mentioning with a beautiful smile.

"You're the new Director, right?" the officer asked her.

"That's right officer, I'm Jaqueline Brambila," she answered him kindly.

"Very nice to meet you, I'm officer Chavez. I'm assigned at the elementary school that's behind the club. Look, just promise me that you'll be more careful when you turn around and I'll keep the ticket, let's leave it in a verbal warning, okay?" At the end of saying that officer Chavez showed her his infractions board where he had a sticker with the team's shield. Without saying anything else, he stopped traffic for Jackie. So, she could cross the avenue without any problem. Jackie's amazement was inevitable for her.

"Thank you very much officer, I promise you it will not happen again." Jackie turned around and entered the parking lot still amazed. It is amazing how people react when they know that Jackie was part of that great soccer team. When she arrived at a store or public place and they saw her wearing an official team shirt, people's attitude changes instantly. Sometimes people were m nicer, and other times they got tougher. Wearing a shirt with a shield from that team really made a difference.

Jackie continued talking with Erik and told him what had happened in the morning with officer Chavez and everything she had felt when she wore the club shirt. At the end of the conversation the managers had already finished eating, and it was time to continue with the pending tasks. Jackie felt that the next step was to remind everyone the excitement of being part of the best soccer team in the city.

Professor Von Zinga raised up from his chair to announce the soccer school had a surprise. It was time to go and find out what was it. The managers innocent expressions did not wait to appear, between laughter and whispers everyone headed towards the clubhouse.

Due to overwork, Jackie hadn't had time to go to the school. She only knew the part where she was having coffee in the morning. Now that they were entering the place she saw all the trophies and awards. She was amazed by so many recognitions and photographs that they kept there.

They did a little tour, there was not much difference with the club itself. You could also see the neglected aspect and lack of maintenance in much part of the building. Although the place where they stopped had something different from everything else, it was precisely in the Little Dragons team dressing room where she felt a significant difference.

"But what a special place Professor," commented Jackie. In this place the emotion has a name and surname, you can feel the pride of belonging to this team. She was saying while seeing all the details that were on that site. The entire dressing room was decorated under the dragon's theme. In the front of each locker was the name of each player in letters that simulated flames. The walls were full of pictures of the team and it had images of the Little Dragons playing soccer all around.

In the center there was a large table, the material with which it was made gave the impression of being a large piece of stone, and in the middle of that great table the uniforms were packed. There were also cardboard boxes which contained sports shoes. Everyone pounded into the packages.

"You see, Jackie! They are looking for their uniforms," Professor Erik commented. Unexpectedly, Martha handled a package to Jackie with her name on it. Smiling Jackie took it and went to the restroom to try it on. It was the first time Jackie wore a soccer uniform.

"It's amazing!" Jackie said aloud. Inside those packages was the complete uniform. Pants, uniform, socks, and a cap. Jackie was rushing to finish dressing and at the same time she was checking each detail of the clothes. What would that stars around the shield mean? The fuss the managers were making made her rush and finish dressing, and finally she came out wearing her uniform. She was one of the last to finish. Almost everyone was already out at the soccer court.

"What do you think Professor?" Jackie showed off her new uniform.

"Astounding Jackie! It looks great on you, but it would probably look better if you put on the proper shoes, you cannot come to the field without them." They laughed. Jackie had forgotten to put the cleats.

All the managers were already on the field, all of them shared that energy, the excitement of wearing those uniforms. That made them feel for the first time in a while, like an excellent team. Despite of having just eaten a couple of minutes before, the work team started to play soccer. Each of them occupied their spot on the arena, they rapidly settled the lodges with for training cones and used only the middle part of the entire area, making the space smaller, but amusing.

Everyone's laughs were extremely contagious, without realizing there were some children form the Little Dragons playing with them. During those minutes it seems like they were children again. but this time they were fun and happy children, instead of whining and spoiled that fought for nonsense stuff. The entire managers team was giving their best effort, they ran, they all jumped towards anything to score, and when that happened, the excitement and celebration were even greater. They celebrated any move, any score no matter what team did it. You could feel the fun at its greatest expression.

"I can't anymore Professor," Jackie gasped at the edge of the cliff. "My mind wants to continue but my body no longer allows it," ere the words that barely raised to say Jackie before sitting on the grass and continue watching the game.

"Pay attention Jackie now that your team is playing watch and tell me. What do you see in them?"

"I just see a blur Professor. Jackie's laughter suddenly exploded. Why? What exactly do I need to see?" Jackie asked him with an uncertainty look.

"Breath Jackie! Feel what you see! They are the same managers from yesterday. They just look different today. They feel different!" Professor Erik exclaimed.

"Yes, they're very different. Now they do look and feel like an excellent team. It doesn't matter who score, or the movements they do, I can detect each of them are making their best effort, and we're all having such a fun time," answered Jackie. "Look at Camila, she does such a big effort when she's running, and she's playing near Ricardo, between the two they are blocking anyone who wants to get to the goal line. I don't know much about soccer but when I play with my children my hands hurt from the bumps of the ball," explained Jackie with a huge smile.

"How can you say you do not know things about soccer Jackie? You made yourself perfect as a goalkeeper, in a natural way. You occupied that place," Erik commented. "Then Jackie, If I may, who told you to place yourself in that position?" Erik asked curious.

Jackie started speaking about how she saw the game. She had a completely unusual form to see things.

"Look Professor from the that place," said Jackie still with an exhausted voice due to her physical effort. "There in the goal area you can see the whole field, you can also throw the ball to the players to score. I realize who is faster, who pulls stronger, and if the other team wants to score at my lodge, I only need opening my eyes to pay more attention. From this position it is easier to figure out the situation. I can open both hands and then catch the ball," Jackie explained her peculiar way of playing soccer. "My youngest son taught me a little secret. He told me, that if I wanted to catch and stop the ball from getting in, I must observe directly into the person who's about to shoot it, and that way I can know where the ball is going," Jackie explained reveling her secrets.

Erik, burst into laughter making Jackie blush. It is amazing how children can teach us so many things. That was the reason why Professor Von Zinga didn't want to change his workplace. That's why he was still in the club. He learned from his dragons, he learned from each one of those children and was certain he had received more knowledge than he could offer. His joys, his laughter, his crying had united him to that team even more than he knew. They used only one equation, there they had a great secret which had led them to be the Little Dragons.

The story that Jackie told Erik had reminded him of an analogous situation he had experienced. Some time ago when Erik was in the middle of a training session with the dragons, the restless Manolo who, had arrived late, needed to make extra ab work as a punishment for his delay. To Erik's surprise Manolo not only did the 50 additional crunches, but also the entire team did twice as they had already established, finished and continued with the rest of the workout.

At that time the Professor was stunned, nor did he know the level of integration that his team had reached. Each of these children has everything necessary to do and achieve anything that they want. When time passes, we forget to feel emotions that make us do things in a fun way. That is why for the Little Dragons there are no limits. They, with their natural way of being, have achieved greater triumphs than the professional soccer team. There is a magical equation, which allows the Little Dragons to take their dreams from the kingdom of dreams and turn them into an incredible reality.

THE DRAGON'S EVOLUTION

After all the chatting and memories shared, the game ended, the managers were exhausted. Some of them even had scratches and a lot of sweat. Everybody went back to the Little Dragons' dressing rooms. Once they all got there they reunited around the big stoned table, moreover Erik started speaking, "Only real members of a real team can sit in this table. Here is where magic happens! Here we all share what happened during a game. In this nest they have learned to fight for what is important, and at this table the best lanes have been made to win several competitions. With this same attitude with which these children have become dragons, now I want to share our biggest secret." Professor Von Zinga got up from his seat and started walking around.

Silence took over the place, everyone was very alert on what he said. Without saying anything else Erik opened from the middle of the table a secret compartment where he took an old board with some sort of formula written on it. With the board in his hands he showed them what it said, "$EE=(e1+e2+e3)^d$"

"What you are looking at is the 'Emotional equation.' This is the magic formula that has evolved our way to feel, see and do things," The Professor explained. "In this we can find 3 ingredients that starts with the letter 'E.' Same ingredients that must be added following the mathematical symbols it has. Emotional energy, plus excellent team, plus exceptional effort. Following that order and summing the first 3 ingredients, we obtain a result. To that result we must add fun. Using our senses, we can capture different sensations, which may come from our own ideas or from where we are. These sensations provide us with a first impression of what we observe and register as first impressions, which are going to be compared with the emotional history that each one of us has, resulting in a traditional thought with a specific emotional charge. This is the simple and practical way to explain our actions. That is why the Little Dragons do what they must do. They have evolved their way of seeing, feeling and doing things. The Little Dragons have in their emotional history positive charges, so when they receive the first impressions their emotional history comes into action and make their thoughts come out strong to face any situation that comes their way. Then we must understand that our behavior is defined by the emotional charge that our thought has caused by one or more sensations captured by our senses," Professor Erik finished explaining.

"Let's see Coach, stop there for a second, and let me understand what I'm listening to. You are saying that many times what I do is the result of my thought?" Martha asked, pausing in the question. "And this thought depends directly on my emotional history that I have registered in my mind?"

"Exactly, Martha. Your actions and those of all of us depend on what our senses capture, compare it with emotional history and according to what it holds is the type of positive or negative charge that is added to your thinking in that precise way and makes you act in this or that mode." Erik breathed deeply and continued saying, "When we have a feeling that has been in our mind for a long time, our behavior is defined by the emotional charge that feeling has. Therefore, our actions show what we feel." Professor Erik looked at them, trying to make himself understood with the ideas he shared.

After a few seconds, an intimidating voice came in asking, "Professor, but that equation seems complicated, it has a lot of numbers and signs that I'm not familiar with, in my case it's going to take a lot of work to fully understand it." It was Francisco's voice, whenever he sees numbers he thinks of something difficult to learn.

Professor Erik moved and began speaking slowly. "This emotional equation, this, which you perceive complicated

Francisco, is the same one you had been using during your childhood, but when you started to grow older you began forgetting it. You stopped using those components that made you and your fellow adventures that secret and invincible squad, able to face anything they had to do," Professor Erik explained looking for everyone to remember the way in which each one of them came to use it in their childhood. It did not take long for one of them to be dazzled by the need to say something.

"That is true, professor," interrupted Jesus Monreal, desperate to talk. "I still recur when I was seven or eight years old the way we managed to get the Chely cow out of the ditch where it had fallen." Without saying anything else, Monreal settled into his chair and began his story. "The elders had given up trying to get the cow Chely without being able to achieve it. It was an exceptionally large dairy cow, it was the only sustenance of don Cyril, that kind grandfather we all wanted, we could not let her be sacrificed. Then Kevin decided to bring the pasture blocks that were in his father's barn. we use all the pasture of the potato at Kevin's house and form Bryan's we took big tables to put them on the blocks of grass. that would make Chely not sink in the mud that was around her, so with a little help from us that huge cow could leave the place. That rescue was known by everyone in the town. I remember that no one could believe it, as a handful of children had done it, we saved the animal. When Chely got out, we all walked together with her by our side, and took her home. We were so happy to have carried out something like that, which the others considered it ridiculously hard," Monreal finished his story

"That is an excellent example Monreal!" Professor Erik cheered. "Look back in your memories those moments in which certain situations caused your emotional energy to explode, see how you and your mates had an excellent team, where you all, with no exception gave their exceptional effort, feel how fun was part of in such a simple way, remember how magical the emotional equation is." This was the practical form that Professor Von Zinga used to finish his explanation about the emotional equation. "This simple equation, unpublished, has evolved the way we act. This equation should be accompanied by more things that make magic happen. Here in our nest, the Little Dragons share our principles. they are only three, but they have been the basis to be able to feel that we see and do." Von Zinga was still speaking as if they were in a ceremony. "Now it is necessary that your mind be open and receptive so that you can feel what you are about to know," he warned everyone.

"Here you have it. The Little Dragons' principles.'

1) Use the emotional equation in everything you do.

2) Understand "we are what we eat and do what we feel". We should feed our body and know our emotions.

3) Foment good habits, they help us to achieve our dreams."

Everyone in that nest was impressed by what they heard, a pleasant atmosphere was created. Those three principles were the basis of a talented team. The Little Dragons were in constant evolution, and those principles were part of them.

"The way in which he has explained the emotional equation and those principles that he uses in his team is impressive. You have made me feel the emotion of being part of the team," commented Jackie.

Erik smiled, the Jackie's comment was quite flattering. "For us it would be an honor to have someone like you in our team. But you must use what you are feeling now to be able to build the team. Here the truly impressive thing is to make the older dragons evolve and do what they must do, wanting to. But to make this philosophy live inside you, you need to feel and do things differently. You need to build your own principles. Hence the visit to the nest is over." Von Zinga, moved thanking for listening and apologizing to them but he needed to prepare to receive his team.

Jackie and all the managers were immersed in their own ideas, then she asked each person to record in their mind what they had learned and to change their clothes to meet her later.

During those days she had received a significant amount of information. She was feeling and seeing things differently. That sensation took her to remember the times in which Dr. Anastasia Deville shared with her the importance of perceiving from another perspective, and how that vision can make a big difference between people.

Jackie stopped for a moment to get out of her bag a booklet of ideas she always had with her, that little notebook was her confidant, when she had an idea she wrote it down there, it was a habit that Dr. Deville had taught her. And now she had written that she must share the emotional equation with her.

She finished writing and continue her path. Then she met Francisco on the stairs He and Martha had been the managers who had enjoyed the game the most. "Hello Francisco, I was glad to see you so animated during the game" commented Jackie touching his shoulder. With a broad smile he answered he hadn't had enough time to enjoy and have fun like that in a while. Confirming that excitement and fun were still present. One of the wishes that Francisco had already fulfilled since joining the club was, to play on the same field where many idols had played.

"Let me tell you, director, that I'm a little tired from all the hustle and bustle, but I feel good about having fun. The talk with Professor Erik was very interesting, but there were times that I didn't understand much about emotions. That emotional charge, it means being loaded with things that happen to us," confessed Francisco to Jackie in secret.

"Yes, Francisco you've understood well. Everything that happens to us has an emotional charge. Tell me how many emotions you think we have?" Questioned Jackie.

Francisco's mouth was half opened before answering. and finally, he said, "Well, I really have no idea, how many are there? Surely a lot." When Jackie saw Francisco's face, she remembered that same question had been asked to her years ago, and her response was very similar. She limited herself to saying that they should be so many that in that moment she could not count them.

"Well then, let me help let me help you a little bit. Let's put a number, and I hope you don't get surprised. There are only four basic emotions," Jackie answered while they got to the last step of the stairs.

"Four, Director?" Francisco yelled doubtful. "Is doubting an emotion? How can we distinguish basic emotions from the enormous emotional cascade we feel every day?"

"That's right Francisco! We've only got 4 basic emotions, and from those 4 we can get a hundred different emotions to come out. Since ancient times they'd been with us. These emotions will help our ancestors survive. The dangers during those times were bigger and more constant."

"Well I do not believe that dangers have diminished Director, on the contrary I believe that now they are a lot more and of all kinds. If you don't believe me, leave the club around eight o'clock at night and you will realize what I am talking about."

"You have a point there! I consider that by costume, fear is the first emotion that makes its appearance in our senses. and we have used it so much that it stayed more than it should. Likewise, there is hate and sadness, they, like fear, are part of our options to feel within the basic emotions that we humans have. But the one that we must keep, is joy, that emotion is the one that costs us the most to find and specially to keep present."

"I get what you're saying Director, but it seems to me that joy is stronger than the other three, you've already seen what happened with everyone a while ago, we were so happy playing as kids. For me emotions are like four sisters, the four always go together everywhere. Pretend they were invited to a party, and only one of the four can dance. While that happens the other three are sitting, in that moment the one who wins is dancing if possible." Francisco was narrating such a peculiar way of seeing all this.

Meanwhile a loud laugh was heard, Francisco had managed to capture in a simple and fun way everything from before. "Well Francisco, so under the example that you put, we must break the habit of always dancing with the ugliest one. If the four are always going to be in all the parties, then you must dance with all of them, but try to do it for the longest time with joy, leaving the others sitting and watching you having fun." Jackie finished her comment following the analogy of Francisco. When she finished she was finally able to enter her office, she had an hour to prepare the next meeting with her team.

The effects from the match at the soccer field were being replicated outside of it. Francisco and Jackie had reinforced what they learned in that meal, the two continued in the same harmony, both were learning from each other. Now she could feel and see that Francisco was evolving more often and his gestures no longer reflected discomfort all the time.

Unconsciously Francisco had already begun to generate a strategic thinking. This type of thinking led him to separate the situation to solve. The not pleasant emotional burden that caused him to not understand some things that Erik said. Nevertheless, this time that strategic thinking led him to break with the costume of being quiet and with that emotional energy and with a little push from Jackie he found his own definition. That impulse that moves us, that internal force that is generated by a strategic thought is called Emotional Energy.

Emotional energy is the first step to start with the process of evolution people should have when they feel and see reality differently.

ALIGNING AN EXCELLENT TEAM

Upon entering her office, Jackie observed her board full of unfinished ideas that she'd left before going to eat. There was one that caught her attention and decided to take it back. It was her strategic development plan. In the first point was to identify the work personality of each manager. For her to know the speed in how they process information and the type of approach they use is of foremost importance. You cannot ask a person to do something they don't know how to do.

In her experience, Jackie had had to face situations with managers who over saw huge responsibilities they didn't even know they attend and had to identify if it was due to overwork or lack of ability to do so. In all companies there were occasions where people knew they had to do certain things. Incredibly, there were places where managers had worked for years and there were things they did not even know were their responsibility and competence.

The emotional equation that Jackie was discovering is related to what she did when interviewing each person that was part of her team in the sports club. To achieve having an Excellent team, it's necessary to know their characteristics, those that form the Work Personality. The set of natural features and work characteristics are what made a person be what he or she is. Characteristics include:

1) The speed in which we understand things

2) The type of approach you use.

Each person reacts and sees things in a different way. The ideas our brain creates sometimes are offset in time related to the moment when they happen, this implies that our brain takes conscience form reality fractions of seconds delayed. Some of us need a few more seconds. But, let us not try to understand that, because that fraction could cost us some more time.

Under the previous framework of reference, we have 3 diverse types of speed to perceive reality, they are:

1.1 Fast

1.2 Slow

Moreover, it happens the same thing with the type of approach (type of attention) we can give that feeling. Let us define tit in only 2 types:

2.1 Directed to the task

2.2 Aimed at people

An Excellent team is the one that is formed by individuals with complemented work personalities, individuals who share the emotional energy, formed form a strategic thinking.

Consequently, these teams would have a better amount of integrated ideas needed for facing any sort of situation in front of them. Let us return to nature and observe how some traits of certain animals can help us to understand in a better way our work personality.

Jackie remembered that class of the month where some occasion there was an exercise in which the behavior of animal clusters that were and cohabited in a single area. It was very interesting for her to see how the pride lions were distanced from the group, restless trying to find the cause to be there.

At the other end of the auditorium were the peacocks, socializing together talking about current issues, that group was always looking to maintain a good image during the time they were in there. What no one knew in that moment was that the class had already begun. At the top of the auditorium was a hidden camera, which was recording them all, their movements, the groups that were forming during the hour they were there.

After that hour of waiting, the instructor who taught the class came in and without giving any sort of explanation began to describe certain animal's features. The bewilderment was reflected on the participants faces. However, after a few minutes they all began to add different points of view about the most important things these animals had.

After debating about animals, the lights were turned off to display a video they had collected during the hour they were waiting (or at least they thought they were just waiting). It became clear how herds and flocks were founding.

To everyone's surprise with this practical training, the teaching has been quite clear. In those moments they were realizing how every time someone expressed their point of view about an animal, what they were really doing was defending their flock or flock to which they belonged. That video was a proof of the existence of the different work personalities, that practical exercise had left a mark on Jackie among with all her companions.

At the end of the presentation a question was exposed, one that covered the entire wall on which it was projected: "Which animal would you identify yourself with? The only way to live with nature is obey it. That set of things that exist in our world produced or evolve without intervention of the human being, that is nature. Obeying nature is a good habit that helps us keep the balance between all the things that surround us. Understanding what our work personality and the people's that part of our work team is and allows us to evolve into an integrated team, where that team understands and enjoys what it does."

Sitting on the red chair of her office, Jackie was still watching the board, full of unfinished ideas, she felt that the equation she was learning was part a math area of her functions. She had always thought that the first thing that had to be understood was people, so that they understand what to do and do it with pleasure.

It looks like a word game where they are all on the board, but they are disorganized, they had to be ordered to obtain an integrated idea. "That's it!" she said shouting excitedly. "We need to give order to all these ideas we need the team to feel and see things from another perspective, Jackie keep saying turning on her computer."

On several occasions during the philosophy courses, Jackie used to borrow her tutor's glasses, Dr. Deville. Dr. Anastacia Deville warmly laughed at that. Jackie did it to let the Doctor see that there was something she didn't understand. And wanted to find in those glasses the Doctor's perspective to always see things differently.

Jackie began writing an email to Dr. Deville. Her professor lived in Berlin, she was about to finish a second PhD in applied philosophy.

"Dear Dr. Deville,

With the pleasure of greeting you, in these few lines Idare to share with you something that has been revealed to me. It is an equation, it has the peculiarity of being an emotional equation, which I consider has the basics to contribute substantially to feel and see things in different form.

I annex the information on the equation and other unified description of the different work personalities that are responsible for its correct application.

Sending you a big hug and trusting that this project will be interesting to you, so I could, as always count on your support.

Regards,
Jackie B."

She sent it and believed that the email had been adequate, it has appropriate words that will help us to sort out what we are facing.

She put her computer aside and continued preparing the next meeting. She took some folders, blank sheets of paper, and diverse color pens. She knew that, in that moment things should be different. While doing so, came another thought to her mind, "Ok, now, what kind of personality do you have Jackie?" Jackie kept processing the information sent to the Doctor, and of course the equation itself.

The work personality each person has in out team could be explained together with the tendency each one has to repeat conducts, so for a certain group of people facing a particular situation, they will tend to react in a relatively predictable and repetitive way. Based on this repetition in patterns of behavior, we can group labor personalities into the following classifications.

LIONS

They use a task-oriented approach, their processing speed is fast. People who have a degree of specialization in what they do. They distribute, order, command tasks to perform. Completely oriented to achieve goals no matter what they must do to accomplish them. This type of personality is characterized by having confidence in their abilities and charisma in order to organize the people who are part of their team in order to achieve the proposed goals. For them, people around serve as means to do things. They are beings who enjoy having control in most of the situations they face.

The Lion's way of thinking focuses on meeting goals regardless of whether they take part in the work.

OWLS

This type of personality has an approach projected in the task, their processing speed is calmer. They look for accuracy. Devoted to perfectionism, they react to the statement, "I tell you how to do it, and you do it." The focus in details is something particular in this group of people. Their thinking is practical, they will always look for the best way to do things without his physical involvement. For them it is very important to have a vast team, avoiding at all costs having an excess of unsolved situations.

PEACOCKS

Their approach is directed to the person, they like to show off their plumage, they have a slow processing speed. Answer the question, "How do I look?" Their thinking focuses on achieving recognition of their own ego. They like extravagance, tend to be disorganized because they are always surrounded by people who help them organizing their life and ideas. They can do many things at once, also get involved anywhere they want, companies use their image.

DOLPHINS

The balanced dolphins have a focus on balance, they maintain a superior speed thanks to their stability. They have the characteristic of being very polite and excellent leaders. Dolphins are equanimous beings, they manage to comply with everything they propose. They are a bit more sentimental than everyone else, sometimes they can act in a reserved way. They are neutral beings with great insight to solve and face any situation that comes their way. In many occasions what motivates them is to offer help to others, their good disposition is always present. They do not like to do things in a hurry, when they feel pressured they look for ways to get more time to adequately fulfill their task.

Jackie knew that knowing the work personality that dominates each of her managers was much easier to find the way to work with them. Thus, achieving to align their personalities with their responsibilities within the club.

As we have seen, a certain group of individuals respond differently to the same stimuli, that is, the way in which they perceive reality makes their behavior variable. It was very common to find working personalities who had no relationship with the position and much less with the functions performed by people in some places.

That was a very difficult task, but to get rid of that something that Jackie had never even imagined would be to find herself in a place where she would have to train a dragon to want to do things. It was something truly out of the ordinary. But in those cases, there was no other way and so she should face the situation. And on this occasion, it had to start different, she had little time to find and apply the principles of the emotional equation.

It was necessary to leave the work personalities pending and to go directly to the project that they had to execute. Each one of us must face our responsibilities with resources that we have in the moment. If you do not find a way to face it, then you are not feeling and seeing things from the right perspective.

LOOKING FOR A STARTING POINT

Before starting the meeting, Jackie met Martha, there was some minutes left before start, however, Jackie saw her and noticed the expression on her causing an immediate curiosity. "Hello Jackie, good afternoon, I just wanted to thank you for the fun time you gave us during lunch, in our area we are always looking for the best option to activate the staff and transmit important information. What we experienced after the meal was something that I did not know, and it made me feel different."

"That's great Martha! But, I have to tell you that we owe those times to the soccer school, Professor Von Zinga and his team were in charge of sharing with us what they have and what has worked for them. Now we must find the best way to use the emotional equation that they shared with us," Jackie finished saying offering Martha chair. "I feel you're different. Martha, is something wrong? Can I help you with something?" asked Jackie

"The reality is that I feel different. Since today I know all those things that have made us lose ourselves and the desire to enjoy our work. Something similar happen with my little son, the thing is that I hadn't had the time to understand it."

When Jackie looked at Martha's posture and voice, she sensed that there was something else from her unexpected visit. "What have you lived with your son?" Jackie encouraged Martha to speak

After listening to that question Martha relaxed her shoulders and decided to share what she thought had helped her see things from another perspective. "Every morning, taking my son to school had become a big issue, making Juanito hurry up and got in time was a big deal," explained Martha. "From waking him up on time, making him wear the uniform, go down to the kitchen, have breakfast, brush his teeth, don't forget his lunch, and be ready before 7 am. It's quite an achievement for a 6-year-old and an odyssey for a mother who must do several things before arriving to work. It was very strange the day we left home on time. The fatigue began to become excessive for me, I arrived at the office late and already tired." Martha explained to Jackie that in her condition as a single mother, she had to take care of many things before starting her day at the club.

After venting a little. Martha finished sharing how her mornings at home have been evolving. She explained the experience of living and learning from a breaking point. She remembered again, and she could even feel the desperation of being sitting there on her staircase at home. The impotence of not being able to change things.

Every morning as soon as the alarm clock sounded, Martha went to Juanito's bedroom. After putting aside, the toys on his bed, she put him on his feet to dress him in the school pants. She left everything ready for the child to finish dressing, then she went down to prepare breakfast and lunch, from the kitchen she was still giving instructions to Juanito, finally Martha came up with breakfast in hand to discover that most of the times her son was not ready yet. How will he be ready if it is so early? He is just a six-year-old boy. There are still many things that a child of that age cannot understand, the first thing he found could distract him. The more Martha did to help him, the later they left home.

Until that day, that early morning when Martha was crying desperately on the stairs. Juanito approached and with his little voice of concern said to his mother, "Mommy don't cry. I want to do what you tell me, but I don't know what to do first and sometimes it takes a long time for me to open the toothpaste, the comb is too high, and I can't reach it. I promise that I will not be so tired anymore. Here, I'll lend you my little cart, so you can also play with it before falling asleep and wake up happy." Martha hugged her son and cried even more. She realized she asked for many things, all at the same time and Juanito did not know what to do. Besides there were so many other things he couldn't do, and of course Juanito went to bed late for playing in the dark with his little cart.

After having lived through this situation, they had to learn from that experience. Things at Martha's were changing and evolving. She had tried to change many times, but she realized it was not the solution. She had to understand that experience in order to start with the evolution process. This process only comes when you learn and learn from a break point.

Now Martha woke up Juanito with kisses, before sleeping both play for a while to wake up happy. They both know what they have to do to be happy and on time every morning. Martha finished to narrate what she did with her son, now she was explaining the relationship that she had found from that.

"I think, Jackie that the first thing is to know what we have to do in specific each one of us and that you also know it. In this way, we are all going to be sure that you expect things from us and us from you," Martha proposed, referring to what she lived with his son. "The facts and knowledge we have must be linked to being able to do so. There are many things that are my responsibility, but the final authorization depends on the company, so sometimes I can not follow things I request in the time required."

Jackie was smiling, what Martha said was what she was looking for. The story she had just heard showed her without a doubt that children are our best teachers. "I completely agree, we need to consider knowledge and power as an essential part of our activities," Jackie told Martha.

Jackie told her what she'd experienced in several occasions when she was inside companies with their "business philosophy" written all over the place, but yet, people didn't know what its purpose was, even less how to put it into practice.

"Here in our club we should do things otherwise. We have been passing through a break point, and we haven't been able to take advantage from it."

"Enough! We need to stop feeling this way, and to make grumpy faces every time we are together in a room. Each of us need to prove one self what we're capable of, and that we are capable of doing things different. We must learn to compare ourselves and no compare ourselves to someone else," Jackie continued, notably enthusiastic and happy. "This that we've just found is the starting point for the club's evolution. These are our principles, and we need to star using them to build a new story, a new way of feeling, see and do things. From this moment on, we are doing what we must do wanting to do so." In Jackie's eyes and voice, one could feel the security she had of finding the bases for the evolution.

Jackie was still overly excited sharing anecdotes with Martha. Suddenly she remembered a phrase that was like "the battle anthem" in a beverages company, where Jackie had worked years ago. The phrase said,

"¡If you do not know how, I'll teach you, If you can't, I'll help you, but If you do not want to! Go back from where you entered because the door is large enough"

"There was the philosophy of terror that moved our actions had an unattainable point of effort, where the lack of respect towards people towards the company itself, and towards them, generated every day unpleasant emotions, which cause individuals to perceive an unsustainable work environment," Jackie finished while moving her fingers to explain this terrible situation. "Now with what we have discovered, we are going to use those refreshing principles but in an evolved way. Martha you have made me remember the first two and now I will share the most important, the wanting to." Jackie and Martha had set up the principles that would give a frame of reference to the actions in the club.

THE PRACTICAL WAY OF MAKING THINGS HAPPEN

Without realizing the time of the meeting had arrived, Martha and Jackie finished talking when they realized that the other managers were coming to the office. Jackie came up with the idea of using the principles that had been established for the team right away, so taking advantage of the minutes before the session started, she began to put pens and benches in each of the managers' places.

When everyone was already in the office, Jackie asked them to take a sheet of paper, put it horizontally in front of them on the table, and divide it into three parts. The first two had to be wider than the last, at the beginning of each part and subsequently they should write down the following: In the center part of the first separation they should write WANT, then in the second KNOW, in the last CAN

It was time to use the principles in a practical way. In the first fragment of the paper they needed to put the approximate time they need to carry out the action that should be noted in the second part of the paper. In that second fragment Jackie asked them to write down everything that everyone was responsible of. They had to list all the things that their area should offer to have a different service to what everyone was used to in the company, but they should not forget to fill out the first part about wanting to do it. In the third and last part, they had to describe in a specific way, how to carry out each of the activities that had previously noted.

Jackie was finishing giving instructions. She wanted everything to be clear enough, in her mind it was clear how each one of them when writing their functions and sharing them with the rest could make all the others participate and create something else with all the important things that would have to be faced to get the solution, but above all, she was looking to make them notice the necessary things to achieve it. They have thirty minutes to do it. Jackie told them, "You must write whatever you consider is the solution to offer the best summer course in the history of this place. You should not write anything else, and you should only use a single sheet of paper." Jackie ended up explaining to make sure that everyone understood the instructions. All the dragons took their sheet and started with the task. Everyone, except Camila.

She didn't do anything at all. Since Jackie gave instructions for the task she watched her with a look of disbelief. A few seconds after Jackie had explained the exercise, Camila raised her voice to say, "Okay, hold on. Let me understand what you want darling. You want that in thirty minutes we put all the things that we must do to offer the best summer course? You must be well misplaced, and I clearly see how you do not have the slightest idea about preparing something like this. One thing is to play but is quite another to insist on wasting our time. What you ask us to do makes no sense. Right now, we have many important things to do. Put aside your games for once and if there's something you don't know how to do, and you want me to write it down for you honey, I'll tell you when I have the time." Camila said with a rather arrogant tone. At the same time, she finished exposing her dissatisfaction, she got up from the chair, without giving Jackie time to say anything, got out of the office arguing to have an important phone call to make.

The voices of everyone began to expand, some of them took advantage of Camila's words about having extra activities and got out of there behind her. Jackie could not believe what was happening, just some minutes before she thought she had the answer to the Club's problems, and now without knowing what happened she was lost once again.

Martha continued in the office, checked her phone because of a buzzing that notified her a new email, she opened it and astonished she read that they had not proceed with the request for the hiring of additional staff for the summer course because they did not agree on the number of new personnel with the number of staff that the finance area had established. Again, the same situation as the previous year was happening, Martha considered important to inform Jackie, she explained the situation and indicated that this would delay the recruitment of staff once again.

In Jackie's face you could see the discomfort and despair she felt, Camila had exceeded any existing tolerance limit. How could she have dared to make the same mistake twice? It was obvious that she had done it deliberately. Jackie left the office decided to put an end to Camila's attitude, went downstairs and got to the finance area.

Her heart rate was accelerated, as did her steps. She quickly arrived at Camila's office, her assistant was not there, the desk was empty and a cup with traces of coffee confirmed it.

Without waiting to be announced, or the return of her assistant, she decided to enter the office. She opened the door abruptly and said, "Hang that phone immediately. I need to speak to you."

"Camila's smile was sarcastic, she did not get what was happening. The "good girl" was now in her role of "bad girl."

"Excuse me Esteban, but the new director has just come in and ask me to hang you up and talk to her." There was a small pause, Esteban was on the other side of the phone he said some words to Camila, then she hung up. "Yes? How can I help you? Why do you interrupt my phone call, and why in the world do you enter my office without knocking?" Camila said watching Jackie standing in front of her.

"I'm here looking to show you how disrespect makes us do things that are not okay. The way you direct yourself towards me is so aggressive and disrespectful, even if you do not want to accept it I am the club director," yelled Jackie visibly upset.

Camila put her hands on the edge of the desk, breathed out and with a movement hit the desk strongly and got up to see her directly into her eyes, "Life itself is very disrespectful dear. In this club your little ideas and methods won't work, you, being here confirms it to me. For the moment you are in a place that does not belong to you, but I assure you that soon you will realize it for yourself and you will leave. Don't get tired trying to find a way to do something for which you are not prepared. Do yourself and us a favor," she said to Jackie aggressively.

The tension was at the limit, it was obvious that Jackie was out of control, Camila surrounded the desk, and both were face to face. In both women their looks were as if they were on fire, their hands moved without control, there was no way to predict the outcome of that confrontation.

BACK TO REALITY

The virtual bell that announced the end of the session had sounded, once again the time was over. One hour and a half session was always to short. They'd already managed having a couple of meetings from distance, technology was very useful to Jackie, it had let her visit Dr. Deville's office several times.

Jackie slowly got up from the couch. She had got her phone connected to the TV in her bedroom, she used headphones that made her listen to Deville clearer. Like it was almost impossible the thousand miles between both.

However, Jackie knew that no matter how many sessions with Dr. Deville, for her it was never enough.

A couple of weeks had passed after the accident, and Jackie felt the fish-in-glass syndrome herself. She just kept on remembering all the things that she stopped doing to look for a future that never came.

During the sessions with her coach Dr. Deville, Jackie had gained a lot of ideas, both had faced and analyzed everything Jackie experienced in the professional and personal field. But how can you make your Dragon Keeper keep working, when it has run out of its internal fire?

Miguel, Jackie's husband, died in an accident Saturday morning. There were no warnings or time for goodbyes. From one day to the next, Jackie had to face the biggest breaking point she had ever felt in her life with her two children.

During the first days she maintained incredulous. The first week she remained ignoring the situation, the support from the club was direct, they gave her a couple of weeks to rest. The second week she stayed away from everyone, she simply wanted to be alone with her two children, she only wanted to protect them from the pain that was around.

The sessions with Dr. Anastacia Deville were escape valves for Jackie, she kept hiding her pain. In her mind there were only those talks she had had with Miguel. The ones Jackie always wanted to avoid and Miguel by some strange reason, insisted in having.

"Never forget my baby, if for some reason I'm not with you anymore, do not let any of the kids suffer for my departure. Explain them that I will always be present in their lives, tell them that part of me will always be with them, and that I'm always going to take care of them from heaven," Jackie remembered what Miguel insistently said to her.

"Enough Miguel stop saying that nonsense! Besides, what makes you think you're going to be in heaven? I'm sure, there is a different place for foolish ones like you". That was Jackie's answer every time her husband talked to her about that.

Jackie had to discover what she would do with her life, there were different options to choose from. She could not continue feeling in a huge pause or pretended to be fine when in fact she felt completely emotionally dejected.

"Feeling good today is inversely proportional to feeling bad for yesterday." With that phrase Dr. Deville was looking to explain the purpose of the session.

"I can't understand what you mean Dr, why is so difficult for you to tell me things directly? Every time you speak to me with those kinds of phrases, makes me feel even more confused," answered Jackie reproachfully. "You do not give an answer, it doesn't make any sense, I have to make a decision and every time I feel more and more unable to do so," continued arguing Jackie by video call. She did not want to understand what had happened. She knew that from one moment to another life broke the balance in her personal quadrant. It was as if the leg of a table had been torn off in one fell swoop and everything that was built on it was staggering.

Jackie had a philosophy of life. She thought that each person's life was divided into four quadrants.

1. The Professional quadrant

2. The Personal quadrant

3. The Family quadrant

4. The Social quadrant.

And each one of them had to maintain a balance.

In the same way that a table needs four legs to sustain itself, the life of any person needs those four areas.

Now Jackie's personal quadrant was incomplete. She could not give her maximum effort in any of the areas of his life.

"There are different levels of effort in the lives of people Jackie, hardly can you maintain a strong and decisive attitude all the time. You have to let yourself slow down," Dr. Anastacia told Jackie. "You must heal your wounds, use a level of effort that allows you to take a break to reorganize your life. The intense use of force is known as effort, when it reaches the highest degree that can be reached is assigned the name of exceptional. The Exceptional Effort has as indicators the level of attitude and aptitude that people show at each moment. That determination or disposition to face situations is known as attitude Knowledge is the ability to develop a certain action called aptitude. Determination and knowledge control the level of effort in which people execute their actions depending on the area they are."

Dr. Deville took her phone from the desk, got up from her place to go and sat in a more comfortable chair, she knew that in those moments Jackie needed a broader explanation of what was happening to her. "All human beings in our life go through diverse levels of effort which can vary directly, due to feelings and emotions that each of us perceive when we face different things. You have to know those levels of effort to be able to evolve them." The doctor finished her comment with a slightly softer voice

"Well let me tell you that the only thing I can perceive at this moment is an intense pain that starts in my chest and disappears in the back of my back," answered Jackie in a broken voice as her eyes began to fill with tears.

In the doctor's face was the despair over not being able to hold her. Anastacia was getting to know a little more about Jackie's life, the emotional connection between them was also increasing, and in the last few days she had worked long and hard to find a way to help her. "Let's do an exercise Jackie." The doctor's mind was designing something to make Jackie feel better. "Walk around the room and find a place where you can comfortably listen to me. When you find it, concentrate on breathing harder, every time air enters your lungs, identify the place in your body where the pain begins."

Jackie had chosen a sofa that allowed her to raise her feet and stay in a horizontal position, without being totally reclining, she put the phone on the bed, closed her eyes and let the doctor's voice invade her mind, "Now with your right hand you are going to touch the place where the pain begins, your fingers should travel in a circular way the area where you feel this intense pain.

When you have drawn a circle in that part of your body, you will begin to tighten your fingers." Dr. Deville couldn't see what Jackie was doing, but she was certain that what she was describing to him, that pain was on the left side of her chest and each time she breathed more strongly, the pain increased.

Pressing the link where she felt the pang of pain with her fingers would let the mind know her body was working to make that unpleasant emotion caused by that situation was diminished considerably. "Continue pressing and feeling where everything comes from, continue with your fingers traveling through the entire area, let them do their work your fingers will heal your body, everything that is hurting. Now change positions. Jackie, move and feel like this new position helps you to reduce the painful feeling, said the doctor." Jackie followed Anastacia's instructions, began to change positions in the sofa, shrugged her feet in the direction of her chest and her whole body changed, resting on her left side, her right hand continued massaging the painful area, her breathing was still strong, however her pain was decreasing.

In Jackie's mind was that word again, that word had always went with her, the comfortable position she had chosen, the pressure of her hand crossing her heart was a mixture of sensations that were taking effect. Dr. Deville paused her talk, letting Jackie enjoy the feeling of comforting herself for a few moments. With this exercise Anastacia tried to make Jackie comprehend the importance of exceptional effort in lives of people. On this occasion, Jackie should assume a different level of effort than she was used to.

Jackie must have understood that attitude is the will that complements us in doing something, and that not only has its application in the working quadrant. Also, there are two types of attitude. The positive, which allows us to face a situation finding a benefit when facing reality with a neutral perception.

And the negative, which stops the individual in the search for some benefit that situation may give, which is why it leads to a feeling of frustration with unfavorable results that does not allow us to reach the established objectives.

Aptitude is formed by knowledge and skill. These words describe the competences of a person, they may seem like synonyms, but when we use a neutral perception, we understand that both are necessary to give.

Knowledge refers concretely to the learning of a person towards the concepts, principles or contents of a sense of what is called, these can be learned through books, academic institutions, and other sources such as the family. Knowledge is the theory and ability is its application.

Ability refers to the skills to use that knowledge and apply it in a practical sense. "Having changed position in the same place, is helping you to reduce the feeling that make something not pleasant and that is dominating your thinking. When we face a break point like the one you're going through, it's highly recommended to pause our activities to ask ourselves and understand these things: what we have? Where are we? And where do we want to go? I am looking for a way to be more direct to give you the tools so you can face the situation in front of your life, but no tool is going to serve you, and nobody will be able to help you if you do not put your ideas in order. Look, first to align the answers to those three questions above. That's what psychologists refer to when they tell you to understand yourself Jackie. Practice in your personal life the business principles that you have shared with me. Complete the knowledge you already have and find a way to give practicality to your breaking point." Deville was doing her best to let Jackie understand her situation. "Use the different levels of exceptional effort so that you have the necessary attitude and aptitude to be able to make the best decision." With that, Anastacia's explanation ended.

During the past sessions Jackie had shared with her the diverse levels of exceptional effort people have, in the same way that she had also spoken to her about different work personalities. Jackie had always kept an exceptional effort in the business positions in which she had developed. She always showed an "iron will" to do things and talent to achieve them.

The different exceptional effort levels are:

Alpha Level: the highest level in its category, here are the people who keep an outstanding determination, within their habits is to have a continuous learning, perhaps the most important indicator is what they do with that learning.

Their talent or rather, their ability to exploit their greatest potential they use to face any situation that comes their way.

Beta level: is a level where people maintain a high attitude or disposition. However, their aptitude is below what is needed to perform a specific activity in an outstanding manner.

Gamma level: this level is characterized by a low level of attitude but has a high knowledge to perform their tasks. This type of people has an outstanding talent, which, in most cases, is overshadowed by their lack of willingness to execute their actions.

Omega level: one of the hardest to evolve. It is a custom for this group to keep a negative attitude in any situation. For this level talking about learning is considered a waste of time. Since their efforts are focused on situations that most times have to do with what other people want for them.

Reaching a different level of effort in the same job position, is something that people must face in order to feat their greatest potential.

"All that Doctor, all that you're saying, I hear it, but I am not listening," Jackie said to Anastacia. For a few moments, Jackie's mind felt the tranquility of the doctor's voice, but for some reason her thoughts are still far from her body. Jackie did not have the will to accept that situation and much less had the knowledge or ability to face it. She thanked Dr. Deville for the time and began to say goodbye.

"Don't worry, Jackie, I have been through a situation similar to yours and I understand perfectly what you are living." The expression on Jackie's face showed surprise, she would never have imagined that behind that distinguished image of Deville's had there would be a story like hers. "By the way Jackie, I want to tell you that before starting this session, I sent you an email essay that I wrote with all the ideas we have faced together, when you feel calmer please open it, in it, you will find what you have explained. But in this occasion, there are more things that complement what you have shared with me. I want that, at the end of this conversation you continue writing as you feel, continue with that habit, I am sure that soon you will find the best way to organize your ideas." Deville sent her a virtual kiss and hung up the phone.

Jackie couldn't contain the tears anymore, knowing that the session was over and that the Doctor could not hear her, she threw herself into bed wrapped in tears, returned to the position she had experienced a few minutes before and began to imagine that someone was still touching her heart but this time there were not her own fingers. She wanted to continue talking to the doctor, in her voice she found the tranquility she needed at that point.

Dr. Anastacia Deville was the only daughter of a Jewish emigrant couple. Anastacia lost her mother at an early age and had to learn in books how her father showed his love. She grew up next to a scientist surrounded by experiments and books.

Her platonic affairs were those great thinkers who shaped humanity. Her beauty was evident, but she looked for a way to stand out for her ideas and not for her physical appearance. That who came to know Anastacia Deville, knew that she was more beautiful inside than outside. Her green eyes like emeralds had a special tone, which in combination with her mind made her shine anywhere she was.

Throughout those weeks she had been talking and supporting Jackie very closely, she could feel a great emotional relationship with her. The essay she prepared had a different nuance to everything she had written before. On those pages were both of their ideas, Anastacia wanted to show Jackie how ordering thoughts led to results that would be simply magical.

In Jackie's email account was that paper that contained the following:

"Dear Jackie, I cannot find words to express my feelings about the situation that you are facing, but I have prepared a few lines that I hope can help you to evolve the breaking points that you're currently living, I have taken charge of ordering all the things that you have shared with me

Now, analyzing the situations that you have talked to me and remembering our telephone conversations, I will explain to you the way in which you can achieve the evolution you need, obviously under business dilemmas.

I can tell you that business evolution is a theory that has a comprehensive operational system which aligns resources of organizations to improve results.

This theory opens the way using strategic thinking, which is guarded by principles and values, making the magic of the emotional equation take effect.

Below, I describe in my own way what can help you to evolve things in the place where you are now.

'BUSSINES EVOLUTION THEORY'

Hypothesis
How to get people to do what they must do. Wanting to?

Objective
Use this theory as a fundamental part in each person's work

Postulates
The formation of strategic thinking

Human beings use our senses all the time to recognize our environment, through the identification of sensations we manage to generate emotions, which are a quick response to that sensation, and it is shown to the outside in the form of an action directed by a thought.

In most cases we face situations by a thought. In the majority of occasions, we face traditional thinking, that is, what we generate without realizing that we are being influenced by our emotional history and by the emotions we have in that moment.

Traditional thinking has three stages and they are:

1. The initial stage in the thinking formation, that is known as the first impression.

During this period, thought formation is generated with a perception of what we observe and with that information we have a quick but incomplete thought.

2. In the second stage that first impression is complemented by the emotional memory that each one of us has. In this case, a comparison is made in which the initial perception generated in the first stage is confirmed or rejected.

3. In the third and final phase an additional emotional charge is assigned to that thought, which will depend directly on the state of the victim that the person has at that precise moment. Resulting in a thought with a certain emotional load.

If you pay attention to the above explanation Jackie you will realize that right now your thoughts contain an extra emotional burden of sadness, so everything else will have that nuance.

You have stayed for a few days with thoughts that have an unpleasant emotional charge, and you have been feeling that same emotion all the time, which has resulted in a physical and emotional exhaustion.

Strategic thinking uses that extra load, to use it for the benefit of the one who is feeling it.

When a strategic thought generates enough energy, a cycle begins in which that emotional energy will be multiplied with each one of its components so that in the end it can explode, making the evolution part of its life.

I will stop using technical words Jackie, I hope you understand with an example that you, yourself said a couple of years ago:

You remember when that amusement park was held in the city where your children live? on that occasion you were late for class, you were very sorry, but very happy. You shared with everyone the beautiful experience you lived in that place.

You snuck into your chair silently and would have managed to go unnoticed if it had not been for the strange noise you made with the balloonfigure you brought in your purse, all blushed, you had no choice but to apologize and explain what happened to you.

Gladly you took from your bag that little toy that was about to run out of air, you told us that it was your son's favorite and that you had won it while playing the hammer challenge, well, now I tell you to remember that challenge and do the same to get out of this emotional state where you are.

In the game of life, sometimes we go through times where it seems we are left without air, but the important thing is that you continue using that hammer with the same intensity to generate the energy that made you win the doll that day. Once again, feel that emotion that caused your child's face, to give a hit and raise that camp to the maximum, ringing the bell that made him jump and jump out of joy.

It was not the force you used, it was the intensity you achieved by directing to the center of the base that blow that made you win the challenge.

Dear Jackie, the intensity of emotions when it comes to strategic thinking helps us overcome any breaking point.

BUSINESS EVOLUTION VALUES

Courage is a very wide concept. It can be assigned to something important or something vague, it can have so many different meanings. What can be important to you, can be irrelevant to someone else, here's the importance of using respect, tolerance and equity as pillars that hold our actions.

Values like:
Respect, tolerance and equity give us the chance to keep an open mind, equilibrated and receptive.

An open, equilibrated and receptive mind give us the business advantage, which let us have the opportunity to generate the strategic thinking that will help us to face and challenge any situation that comes our way.

Every human being perceive reality in a different form. Respecting opinions, ideas or actions from others, help us to get the necessary equity for our workplace and labor surroundings by tolerating an idea, an opinion or maybe an action.

BUSINESS EVOLUTION PRINCIPLES

Principles are rules that determine people's actions. In this theory business principles are shown, those that are the beginning point for people to face the several types of situations they have in front and need a solution.

Wanting, knowing and being able are the principles that give its shape to this theory. To want: is the beginning of any human action. To Know, is having the sufficient knowledge. To be able to (or can), is using the sufficient force to achieve the necessary intensity for evolving or developing things.

Emotional equation

I made some changes to that magical formula you have sent Jackie, and I would like to explain myself. Firstly, it is quite simple, but modifies the intensity in a very significant way. You just need to change the mathematical sign that you join to the equation and instead of adding you must multiply.

By multiplying you can increase the force every single ingredient has, obtaining its greatest strength and finally when you square everything with fun, it generates some sort of emotional bomb that makes people achieve any goal they intend. So, at last, the emotional equation goes like this:

$$EE = (e_1 \times e_2 \times e_3) \, f \, / \, t$$

Secondly, as you can see the second change I made, has to do with one ingredient that allows us to measure the duration of a determined period in which an action is carried out. That ingredient is known as time. Mr. time has to be present in the equation, he's who has always determined the period of things.

Therefore, by multiplying you increase the strength of each element, you're still raising everything with fun and now you get to spot a specific period of time to accomplish. You can't forget Jackie, the most important thing about this theory is making it a part of your life, a part of you.

Remember that, the key to break with some bad costumes is using good habits which help you for the evolution in our present. I hope this will be to your liking, the way I have organized your ideas. I send you a huge kiss and my best thoughts to help you in this process.

Don't forget to think about my proposal, I really want you to come and visit. Make a parenthesis in your life, and seek to breathe new airs, I assure you that it will help you in the search for your balance. Remember that, strategic thinking is what you need to face your new life.

Moreover, the concepts that both friends had been exchanging what Dr. Deville was trying to explain by ordering Jackie's ideas was a supported theory indifferent postulates as a frame of reference to achieve the goal that she had found in Jackie's thoughts.

'The secret to this approach was based in gathering the necessary ingredients to evolve the way of feeling, seeing and doing things.

Love, Anastacia Deville"

Anastacia Deville was accommodating the column vertebrae of this theory. Along with Jackie, was connecting the arteries to give the first beat of her new business heart.

SHOTS LEAVE THE HEART ONLY THE SOUL CAN LODGE

Jackie had succeeded to fall asleep after drowning her pain in her own tears. The days that the club had given her had ended. She must continue with her life exactly where she had left it. The next day, early in the morning, she finished saving Miguel's belongings in boxes, got out of the bedroom and prepared breakfast for her children. To her surprise they were already in the kitchen finishing serving fruit with honey that Jackie liked to have for breakfast, the face of both children lit up when they saw their mother laugh for the first time in days.

Fausto, Jackie's youngest son had his little face full of honey, that same honey he had used to decorate the dish at the same time he was tasting it. "Mummy, your breakfast is ready, I was just trying it, to see if the honey was sweet like you like it." The laughter of all invaded the kitchen, and the only Jackie could do was to approach them and give them a sticky hug. That day she went back to enjoy her children feeling less pain than the previous days.

After having taken a hot shower, and dressed casually, she left her house for the sports club where they were already impatient to see her. From the moment she arrived at the parking lot, the displays of affection began, when she arrived at her office, Alexia's spontaneous hug made her sit for a moment in the waiting room.

After breathing in and out and having cleansed the tears that had sprouted she decided to go back to her office. On the table there were several boxes containing various details that the managers had left. Jackie watched them from a distance without noticing what they were. She turned on the computer and turned his gaze to the table, decided to get up from his chair to verify what those boxes contained.

When he got a little closer to the table she could see that there was a red folder on top of all of them. That piece of paper contained a couple of paragraphs that had made Jackie touch her heart again with the fingers, then she took the folder, opened it and without thinking anything began to read it:

"Dear director:

The whole team wants to share with you a part of them. for us to have given us your ideas, to have shared your experience, everything has left something that no school could have given us. No matter how long you have been here with us, you, with your energy has helped us feel and see different things. for which we wanted to offer some details that could help you in these tough times.

We know that making a gift is usually difficult, and even more so when someone goes through a situation as unexpected as what you live. Even so, what is in these boxes represents for each one something valuable, something symbolic and special that has made us dare to give it to you in the same way that you did with us. Please, take these gifts as a sign of our respect and admiration."

When Jackie finished reading, she had to sit down because of the emotion it caused in her. She was receiving several emotive shots the heart of all her dragons. She took the first box that was near and with extreme care began to open it. It was a white box of a hexagonal shape. When she finally managed to open it, she saw a piece of paper folded in the same shape as the box that contained it.

There was another thing inside, when she started unfolding, she felt an electrifying sensation running through her hands and then her whole body.

"Dear Jackie.

After looking through my stuff and also looking around a lot of different places a gift that could combine with you, I decided to give you a prayer that has been locked in my mind for a long time, and now is time for it to come out and help you.

I had used these ideas but, separated several times, and now with your help I realize I must feel them altogether. I consider these thoughts needed to face any break point we have in our lives.

Please read them aloud and if they achieve to have an effect in you, share them with your love ones.

Father, you are in my heart

You, who are part of my life

I ask you for the strength to move forward and resist

I raise this prayer to you thanking your company

Share with me your love, justice and temperance

Give me the opportunity to bend without breaking

Allow my soul to save its balance

Help my spirit find its place

Do not let evil invade my thoughts

And walk with me the road to happiness."

When Jackie finished reading, she felt absolutely identified with that, it was as if someone knew exactly what Jackie needed. That one soul who wrote those lines was exposed in front of her. The first shot had caused an enormous impact to her heart.

Jackie realized that the gift hadn't got any signature or name, so she could know who was the present from, she continued opening the next box and realized that one didn't have any remittent either. In those moments her thoughts were interrupted by the phone's sound on her desk, she rushed to answer.

"Director I hope I'm not interrupting anything." It was Alexia who was on the other side of the phone. "I just wanted to say, that I hope you are opening all your presents, by decision from the entire team, none of the presents have the name of the person who gives it to you." Alexia finished saying that and hung up.

Jackie was still with that piece of paper in her hands, she thought those dragons had given her something she would have never imagined. There were more boxes on the table. Jackie was experiencing the total opposite to what she had felt in previous days. They were the same kind of boxes, where hours before she had stored her memories, now when she was opening them she was feeling the energy that had been given.

When we decide to open our mind and share a little of how much life has given to us, the sensation we get is indescribable. That sensation always manifests itself in your senses. The one who enjoys giving and the one who receives is filled with the energy that the other has decided to share. That is the purpose of offering a gift.

Suddenly Jackie noticed that there was a box that she had not seen before, it caught her intention instantly, it was bright blue and white, when she was closer to her and could take it, she realized that the package looked like a block of ice. When she opened the box and found a blue book inside, her curiosity was abrupt. She made space on the table, prepared a cup of hot tea and began to open it with great emotion. It was a manuscript that was accompanied by bluish-white leaves when she started to look through it. She realized that the book has a mixture of old texts and recent sheets that made it even more interesting. Jackie took a sip of her tea and started to read it:

"The great lords of ice."

During the time that we have inhabited these lands we have witnessed how certain people have marked and conditioned destiny of men. Many have been the stories that my mother told me about those great empires formed by vast tracts of land. I had always asked myself.

Why do men seek to conquer other places?

Now, far from home I allow myself to remember all the manuscripts I had read, all the memories that my mother shared with me, many times I struggled to understand what she was saying, some stories were incomprehensible to me in those times, I just enjoyed the sound of her voice and the way I settled into her lap.

When my father was at home, I asked him to tell me about the places he had been and all the things he had lived. He smiled, took me in his arms to carry me to the height of his chest. I listened to him until his voice went away in my thoughts when he kept quiet and opened my eyes, so he could continue talking to me.

Much of my childhood I enjoyed inside my mind, some months of the year the weather was quite extreme, and my mother would not let me go out to enjoy the forest. I always knew places through my father's eyes, and with his stories I built my future. I grew up among weapons, horses and expeditions.

I learned horseback riding before walking, my best toy was my father's shield, that huge shield that many times helped me to stay under his meeting table without anyone seeing me. There I kept a long time without moving a single muscle of my body, I was bewitched to hear those stories about people who disappeared from the map in a matter of days.

People who seek their growth simply by invading others is destined to defeat. People that builds a civilization based on the development of its people, will always have an enormous advantage that will take them by their nature to conquer those places that do not know the internal fire. This internal fire makes us achieve victory as part of our destiny.

Our men and women shared this secret equally, all people in our town used it. Since you were a child they sowed it in you and when you were ready you could demonstrate your strength. But first, you have to develop, then make it grow with your warrior spirit. This simple way of seeing life was what my father was in charge of teaching.

We knew in what time of the year we had to dedicate ourselves to develop our strength and at what moment we could go out and try it Ice and snow were part of my life; the cold was my ally. In our culture we know that all beings that exist on earth are in some way connected to mother nature. This union is best explained when we share the idea about the useful nature of our people. This helpful nature helps us to understand that every living being serves something or has a particular function. Each one of us must find the nature of his being, learn to develop it and when the time is right to demonstrate his strength.

In the useful nature of our ice civilization, nothing exists just by the fact of existing. Everything that is felt is thought and done, has a relationship or makes sense with the internal fire. When ice is all over, the only choice you have is learning how to become a part of it. Learning to survive in those conditions without loosing your essence is something our people always kept.

These permanent and invariable characteristics determine what we are. When you find yourself surrounded by solid nature, you got to learn that your own essence is solid enough to become part of it, otherwise you would die in the process. Our civilization has been formed with the purest heat that can exist. That heat feeds our internal fire, that food is provided by our family and each family is part of the helpful nature of our civilization. In our helpful nature, my family had a lot of things to do, every journey my father did represented an advance in our destiny.

I can still remember him saying, "Our destiny is guided by our thoughts." When your thoughts have the warrior spirit, there's nothing nor nobody that could stand in your way, nothing but yourself. The warrior spirit and essence were a part of our thoughts. "We must always have a strong thinking, so strong that our enemies can feel them and tremble in the distance" For many years our civilization showed that strength among the rest of the townships.

Due to my inherited nature from my mother, I had always wanted to travel and conquer in a different form, I dream with knowing new and far places where I could show our culture's greatness with no blood spilled. Of course, I had to hide my feelings and made them grow in another way, during those moths at home, things happened in an unexpected way for me.

When that time came to an end I was there, but because of my father's orders I kept my distance form battle, my body was far away, but my soul was present that day in that place. Safe, and feeling secured owing to the ship, I had no choice rather than to hold in my memory all those ideas. I was seeing my people's destiny, I was waiting for the sign to initiate the journey that would led us end those lands conquest.

Around my ship were more than 500 war crafts, all ready to accomplish our destiny. From distance you could have seen my father's personal squad, always faithful, always so strong and ready to continue. There were more than twenty lines of huge bears, warriors that wielded their heavy and pointed spears, willing to start the conquest. With a few miles ahead, the horses had already begun the trip, those warriors displayed great ability in battle. That made them seem merged, horse and man, they seem like one.

A week before we had devastated with the north coast of that island, the formation of disembarkation caused extreme fear among them, they had never seen a warrior fleet of such magnitude. Anyone who had been present at our arrival would have run away terrified and begged for their soul.

With the disembarkation of the first line was more than enough, we walked on the sand on top of their bones, that day throughout evening you could see the reflection of their red blood all over the beach, there was no captures, the order was direct, we had to eliminate everything and everyone in that place. We only let some of them see our arrival and ran away terrified, confirming that "The great lords of ice" were there to conquer their lands.

The first third of our fleet was on land, we had to use the triangle of power to advance all together and arrive at the same time 300 miles ahead. Next to me followed the warrior ships loaded with howling wolves, waiting for the legacy of the full moon, the left beak of the triangle had to be strengthened, once we had advanced through its waters surrounding its lands, these warriors would rush upon our enemy causing a mortal wound in their ranks.

Horses will go by the trickiest side, but also the one that will cause the most harm, the power of their mounts and the certainty of their arrows would form a rain of fire that would finish closing the right peak of our triangle of power, and the spirit of struggle of all our men had flooded their whole being. Bears, wolves, and horses were part of the warrior nature of our army, the strength of our essence crowned the soul of each one of them.

Dawn is breaking, the moment had arrived but there was something that appeared in front of the triangle that made my spirit tremble with uncertainty about what I was about to contemplate."

Jackie couldn't stop reading that blue book. She, like most people, did not know everything that was behind that great civilization. When she was about to start reading the part of the manuscripts, the sound of the door opening caused here to jump, "Hi, Jackie, good afternoon. Your assistant is not here, so I knocked a couple of times, but you didn't answer." It was Esteban arriving to her office.

"Hello Esteban, come in, welcome. Sorry I didn't hear anything, come, have a seat please." Jackie said pointed at the chairs. Esteban was doing a courtesy visit to Jackie, as his boss, he had to offer condolences on behalf of the entire group. He chose the chair that was near the window, took a seat and waited for Jackie to approach.

"Everyone in the group is dismayed about the situation that you are going through and we want to offer you total support for you and your family to move forward, as you know we have the resources and the means that we put at your service for the care of your children, as soon as you decide it please talk to the human capital area to find the best way to support you,"

Esteban explained in a comforting voice. "I have no arguments or words to help you with all this, yet I want you to know that I share with you the pain of having lost a loved one and I understand what you are suffering. Maybe it is not time to say it, but in my particular case, continuing to work with the pending things helped me remain strong." Esteban was looking for a way to offer Jackie some comfort.

Things at the club had followed the course Jackie had driven, the summer course was already there, internally there were still many things to be fixed but in general terms life there continued. Esteban sensed that he should inject encouragement to Jackie to make her continue with her working life and of course he didn't want to lose a valuable element like Jackie in his team. Despite notknowing what was happening at the club exactly, whatever it was, Jackie was the one doing it.

The conversation lasted a few minutes more, hewas showing some discomfort for not knowing what to say, he didn't want Jackie to leave her job, but neither did he wanted to force her continue. He had to let her take the decision. When he was almost out of the office, he approached Jackie to say goodbye, gave her a hug and told her that he had also left a gift at the table. Jackie, a little dismayed by Esteban's words, decided to open the window and breathe deeply, trying to calm down again.

Before arriving at the club and discovering those gifts, her mind was clouded by excessive emotions. There were too many blamesshe did towards herself.

Jackie had looked for the way to conquer new horizons, but she never imagined what this occasion destiny would show her. In her thoughts and behind the pain she felt there was the clarity she needed to know the reality of her situation. In those moments and in spite of all the emotions found, Jackie wanted to continue discovering that energy she was finding when she opened the gifts. So, she went back to it, and continued with the blue book that she was so enjoying. There was something in that writing that made her feel identified with the great lords of ice and return to her reading:

"The cloud of dust that was forming in front of them was unmistakable, it was a sign of what was about to happen. At that moment we were all witnesses of how our enemies arrived so unexpectedly. The opposing army was there in such a surprising way, they must have traveled at night and without rest to have covered that distance in a few days.

During those moments my mind detached itself from my body, in an accelerated way I climbed to the tip of the ship's mast, I needed to confirm what was happening. I lost sense of time, from that moment everything happened slowly, I still hear the horn announcing the battle.

From my position I managed to see how a small barge coming from the ship closest to the coast left for the mainland in search of an emissary. All the ships were anchored still and in position to strike, we could not move as fast as we would have liked.

In that situation of total impotence, we saw the way in which the last battle that changed the course of our history began. Without waiting anymore, I felt a strong shake caused by the unfolding of the sails, and at the same time a small movement that ended in a collision with the hull of another ship, in spite of this we could not advance, we had to wait until most of the fleet moved to try to get closer to the coast.

My mind suddenly returned to my body to give me that pain. In the distance the placement of the enemy forces can be observed, they passed so close to me, those big fire balls that they began to throw to our ships, the closeness of each other made the attack more accurate.

How was it possible that our gods allowed that? In front of my eyes fell our imposing empire. Between fire and dust, I came to see what the most painful moment of my life has been. The personal troop of my father was no longer waving nor fighting, it was unconceivable, both for me and for the rest of the fleet.

Our beloved king had succumbed in battle, he, just as his faithful warriors had had the fortune to end his existence by doing what his nature commanded.

The pain I felt was so intense that it made me bend. For several minutes I was speechless, at that moment the emissary my father had sent arrived, as soon as he saw me he pounced on me to give me my father's shield, he had wrapped it in one of his cloaks and entrusted it with his life to give it to me. The next thing I heard was the sound that split my heart in half, the warhorse announcing the retreat.

I had to be held, so I would not run in search of what I thought was my destiny. the noise around me was shocking, the heat caused by the fire caused our ships to succumb one by one.

The last thing I can remember, is my own image embracing the cape that was given to me, before losing consciousness and sinking into the pain of defeat. Our gods stopped at sunrise and guided our souls to make our way in that hell. The strength of the god of thunder was present on the horizon, I could feel his energy that lifted me, releasing my soul from my body in the prow of the ship.

My prayers had been heard, I had started the journey that any warrior wanted, the father of all had sent his beloved son to show me the way. During those moments I managed to find the answer to all my questions. I managed to understand how nature of men dictates their destiny, how a thought that is guarded with the spirit of struggle, and strength of its essence does not let bind to fear.

Fear could not spread, simply because it is not part of our thinking, and there was the explanation to the phrase that bred with me, "Our destiny is guided by our thoughts." I must have a strong thought, sustained with my spirit of struggle so that the nature of my being dictates the way. Nature overflows me, and it is the same that reminds me of my mother explaining what love is, she demanded it from the sacred books of her god, where the phrase "that you love one another, even as I have loved you" was repeated several times.

Here are the 3 guidelines from the triangle of happiness my mother taught me:

Love: is the fifth element that exists in nature, it surrounds us at all times without even realize it, when someone discovers it and decides to take it, it evolves inside in the form of a feeling.

Passion: the overflowing emotion that makes one enjoys love for an action, thing or person.

Balance: the alignment of emotions, without giving nor receiving much. Everything must be in place to reach and harmonize things around.

Loving is an action that must balance love and passion, so we can obtain happiness. Happiness in loving what you do. My mother has love for knowledge and passion for lecture, that made her conquer her own happiness, still knowing that my father's passion was war, and that it would let him to exactly what I was going through.

When the nature of struggle merges with the passion for war, any warrior finds happiness by ending their days on the battlefield. My father and all his men were sure that such an end would be rewarded by the gods. After listening to my own thoughts, the God of thunder could feel the power of my essence, fighting to find my own nature so it'll be the one showing me the way. So, from an accurate blow, he sent me back to my devastated body.

With that help, I managed to return to reality, it took me a few minutes to feel the strength of my inner strength going through my body, when I managed to open my eyes, the brightness of the sun caused confusion in my mind. If it had not been for the fact that I was still hugging my father's cloak, I would have thought that it had all been a bad dream.

When I finally managed to stand up, the men around me exhibited a look of wonder, none of them dared to say anything, but I knew that they identified my body had accompanied my father when they saw me immobile on the floor. As soon as everyone was aware again of my presence that group of men and me, together we asked the father for all for his protection and consolation for what had happened.

We were surrounding the northern part of that island, our first point of arrival was the Faroe Islands, there we could recover forces to continue with that new hard journey. My destiny was taking a complete turn, we no longer returned home defeated, now we were heading to the opposite side, our spirit of struggle and the passion to know new lands.

When I looked down I noticed that my rips were stained with blood, so I decided to use what I was carrying, I felt a huge need to cover my back with my father's cloak, I walked a few steps towards the side of the mast were there was a little stockroom, and inside I began to uncloak that great shield that was now mine.

When the shield was exposed I remember how to use it, I knew that a shield gave protection, but you must not use it all the time, the shield protects the body and the sword allows you to advance in battle. With my arms I took the shield hugging it and with the cape on my back I managed to reach my internal fire, which caused me to remember the strength that my father was projecting when he used them, in that embrace I gave the promise to continue with the nature of my destinationwhatever it was.

When I put the shield next to me while lying on the floor, I could see a small indentation on the inside. For a moment I thought it was stuck in a dent but observing it more in detail and touching that part I could feel that it was a kind of relief on the inside, which had been exposed as a double cover for the leather that worked as a lining.

I began to touch these reliefs with the tips of my fingers, and I realized it had something engraved, an indescribable sensation ran through my body. I knew that what I was about to discover was something my father wanted me to remember, by removing the lining completely I was able to see an engraving written in runes.

'The fire of the eternal dragon'

This phrase was carved around the edge of the shield, a little lower was the image of the knot of power too, behind the triangles was a baculum, in that image there were also a couple of circles, it was a traditional symbol that I knew from eternity. Those carving showed traits of having been hidden for a long time, I could feel the hardness of the earth around them, using my fingers I began to clean what I had in my hands little by little I discovered the engraving in its entirety.

Between the earth that I was removing I could see there were more elements in that image, there was no doubt, those two circles showed a silhouette of Hugin and Munin those two crows that always accompany the father of everything. Hugin is the thought and Munin is the memory, both are guarding the power knot. I had a larger triangle that framed the knot, in the centerwas a small hole that showed me a bright red jewel.

My surprise was immediate, I was contemplating for the first time a traditional symbol exposed in all its splendor. I had on my hands our civilization, our town, our culture, this is the treasure my father had always talked about. In my mind all the pieces were settling.

The 3 interlaced triangles stand for the fusion of essence. Nature and the warrior spirit in the middle in bright red is where the soul is found. The power of the inside fire keeps the soul lighten, the interlaced triangles must stay balanced to make the baculum of strength behind them work. Thoughts and memory should be always there, so they'd be who guide our destiny.

Father of all, immersed in the power of the ocean and surrounded by the cold that feeds my body, I swear allegiance to the power that you are hitting in me. Allow the strength of the elements to guide me and you, to be my path. There was no more pain inside, I felt the shield's protection gathering my soul.

I finally understood "the knot of power force", that force has been always scratching my insides, now it is breaking into my thoughts to make them grow, I have never grown so beautifully grievous. For our enemies that battle was the end of an era. For me, those moments were the endurance of our legacy.

Many rushed to say that my days had ended with my father's country, but few were those who were present in the dragon's exile. My name is Maria Haraldsdotter, legitimate heiress of the great lords of ice, and this is the beginning of my story."

Jackie was shocked, it was a woman all the time. She immediately looked for more information, and her surprise was even bigger when she found, Maria's Haraldsdotter date of death was register the same day her father died. Maria was the first princess of ice who received a name in another culture. And that story Jackie had read was the last battle of an era.

The first part of the blue book had ended, that explanation of those engravings, that short story caused such an admiration in Jackie towards the narrator, Maria Haraldsdotter, that she wanted to learn more about that civilization. Those gifts came in the right moment. Jackie had struggled to make good progress in the professional quadrant, but at the same time there was the family quadrant, her children would need comfort and guidance in the face of their father's loss. Life took her to a breaking point where she could not change things. Where can Jackie make the biggest contribution? In this period of time, Jackie was getting back to reality after the lecture. She took her notepad and wrote down 2 only options:

1. Continue working at the cub, focusing on finishing her projects, applying her philosophy and using her principles as guidance in her labor quadrant.

2. Focus on her family quadrant and return to her children and their hometown where the rest of her family lived. They could help her in this new chapter of her life.

Business Evolution takes you back to the place where each of us know, can and want to be at.

EPILOGUE

In the last couple of weeks things have changed at the club, nevertheless from my point of view it hasn't been just because of Jackie's ideas. In fact, I can tell you that her absence has been beneficial to all of us. I have always thought you cannot send a frightened person to do a leader's job.

The theoretical part Jackie knows is true and real and it has been important but putting that into practice has been on us; it's our responsibility. Yes, it is in fact that I should accept that respect and tolerance have helped me overcome things, keep calm and turn different my way of thinking.

These weeks that Jackie has been out of the club has been long and boring. Now I understand when I listen to people say: there's no day without night. Jackie owned the theory, but she requires more practice, she's got some great ideas, but she lacks strength.

When this book came into my hands, I felt once again the intensity in which every single thing happened. We were never the perfect team, but I can assure you, that, as well as us, you have also been using the emotional equation.

The magic from the little dragons contributed directly, so I could know a unique way to do things. Martha, with her extreme sentimentalism made me realize that most of the times, it isn't that you don't want to do things, but it's simply not possible to do them because of all the bureaucratic garbage around us.

We have been taught, numbers are cold, words are boring. When you have a goal to carry out you should use everything that is in your hands to make things happen. This business theory is part of the tools that open the path in everything we do. Let's remember that words become images that is why, right here and right now a powerful and strong trident is falling down into your hands. This trident would help you break with costumes that dominate our actions.

None of these words written here would work if you don't have the force and the courage to accomplish whatever you want to accomplish. The trident couldn't appear without a strategic thinking, and that thinking wouldn't been strategic if it was not accompanied by principles and values guiding everything in our life.

When you face a break point you must have something that helps you continue the battle. Every company, every enterprise needs this, this practical form of aligning the resources in all types of organizations, small or big, in order to have better results, this is what we have named CEO System.

Life is disrespectful, and Mr. Time rides with no rest at all, any day, an obstacle could appear right in front of you. Who knows? Maybe even in another dimension. Past only exists when we remember it. We should realize we have as a costume living our present with feelings from our past, and those emotions make it harder to build our future. Bad costumes can only disappear with good habits.

And you? How do you live your present and how do you continue building your future?

WORK PERSONALITY

During business evolution of any organization it's highly important to know the labor personality of people in the work team. Here, you will find a set of questions that will help you discovering yours.

Objective: knowing your personality in the way you relate with others at a working environment

Instructions: you must read each question calmly. Then identify which of the 4 phrases describe your actions and way of thinking better. You need to choose only one option for each question.

1. At work do you want to be recognized by?
( ) Your productivity
( ) Your contribution
( ) Your involvement
( ) The quality of your work

2. When you are in a work team as you usually are?
( ) The leader, you have control
( ) You look for harmony, be the center of attention
( ) The mediator feels included
( ) Information provider

3. How do you like to work?
( ) Intense, focused, do several things at once
( ) Free, interacting with a lot of people
( ) Cooperative, polite
( ) Careful attentive to details, one thing at a time

4. What is it that motivates you when you are working?
( ) The results
( ) The recognition
( ) Help others
( ) The activity itself

5. How fast do you talk to your coworkers?
( ) Amazingly fast
( ) Fast
( ) Slower
( ) Moderate

6. How do you like to dress when you are in the company?
( ) Good taste, formal, elegant
( ) Strong colors but moderate
( ) Soft, casual, muted colors
( ) Conservative, traditional

7. What is your way of communicating?
( ) Direct to the point
( ) Animated-impulsive
( ) Patient
( ) Focus on the details

8. How do you organize your office?
( ) Everything is organized by priorities
( ) Very orderly disordered
( ) Few papers, just the necessary
( ) Many papers, in ordered heaps

9. Which is the speed with which you like to work?
( ) Very fast, a fast whirlwind
( ) Fast enough, you get bored easily
( ) Without hurry, you dislike the methodical pressures
( ) Very steady pace

10. What moves you?
( ) The pressures, the changes
( ) The interesting things, the fun
( ) The companionship, the support
( ) The precision, the information

11. What is bothering you the most when you are working?
( ) Waste time
( ) Doing what has already been done before
( ) The confrontation
( ) Being wrong

12. What do you want to receive in exchange for granting your maximum effort in the company?
( ) Power
( ) Recognition
( ) Approval
( ) Responsibility

13. What do you like to talk with your companions?
( ) About achievements, results
( ) Dreams and aspirations
( ) Feelings and experiences
( ) Data and amounts

14. When do you get upset, as you show?
( ) Impatient and aggressive
( ) Frustrated, you can burst
( ) Confused but gentle
( ) You don't really get angry that easily

You must not forget that these questions are simply a guide, the reality of your personality you carry within you and have been evolving every time you face a breaking point. For more information on your labor personality and more tools that will help you to understand and to increase your labor quality enter our website www.business-institute.org

www.ingramcontent.com/pod-product-compliance
Lightning Source LLC
Chambersburg PA
CBHW030759180526
45163CB00003B/1085